BEA WEHRLY

Counseling Interracial Individuals and Families

AMERICAN
COUNSELING
ASSOCIATION

5999 Stevenson Avenue
Alexandria, VA 22304-3300

10 9 8 7 6 5 4 3 2 1

American Counseling Association
5999 Stevenson Avenue
Alexandria, VA 22304

Acquisitions and Development Editor
Carolyn Baker

Managing Editor
Michael Comlish

Cover design by Brian Gallagher

Library of Congress Cataloging-in-Publication Data
Wehrly, Bea, 1926–
      Counseling interracial individuals and families / Bea Wehrly.
         p.   cm.
      Includes bibliographical references and index.
      ISBN 1-55620-154-0
      1. Cross-cultural counseling—United States.   2. Minorities—
Counseling of—United States.   3. Counseling—United States.
I. Title.
BF637.C6W387   1996
158′.3′08904—dc20   96-11767
                                                                                          CIP

CONTENTS

PREFACE

The interracial population of the United States has undergone such a dramatic increase in the past two decades that authors are proposing that the "face" of our country is being transformed and that this transformation will bring a new meaning to race. In spite of this increase, the counseling profession has given minimal attention to the interracial population. This book introduces counselors to the needs and strengths of individuals and families with more than one racial heritage and suggests counseling interventions that are appropriate for use with these people.

Chapter 1 familiarizes readers with the interracial population and provides a rationale for counselor attention to interracial individuals and to people in interracial relationships.

Chapter 2 underscores challenges that interracial people face in developing a racial/cultural/ethnic identity. Historic perspectives on interracial identity development are also reviewed in this chapter.

Chapter 3 provides general guidelines for counseling with interracial individuals and families. Emphasis is placed on counselor self-awareness of values, attitudes, and behaviors toward the interracial population as a vital first step in counseling these people. Process guidelines for counseling interventions with individuals and families with more than one racial heritage are also included in Chapter 3.

Chapters 4, 5, and 6 include a developmental focus for counseling interracial children, adolescents, and adults. Content in each of the three chapters is addressed for the respective developmental level under the topics of counselor self-awareness, issues faced, contemporary perspectives on racial/cultural/ethnic identity development, and counselor roles. Case studies are included to illustrate counselor roles with interracial individuals at the developmental levels addressed. Chapters 4 and 5 also contain considerations for counseling interracial adolescents in foster or adoptive homes.

Chapter 7 introduces readers to interracial family counseling issues, discusses counseling interventions appropriate for this population, and includes a case study relating counselor roles and techniques to use with an interracial family. This chapter also includes considerations for work with families that have become interracial through cross-racial adoption or cross-racial foster home care.

Chapter 8 addresses challenges that counselors face in helping interracial individuals to move beyond the "Other" status.

Ideally, readers will find the time to peruse all of the chapters in this book. I recognize, however, that time limitations and special interests sometimes lead to reading one or two chapters only. Because of the possibility that readers may limit their reading to single chapters, Chapters 4, 5, 6, and 7 each contain a section emphasizing the importance of counselor self-awareness as the first step in counseling interracial individuals. Readers studying all four of these chapters may find this section redundant after the first reading and choose to move to the section that follows. This information was included in all four chapters to underscore the critical importance of counselor self-awareness of issues that could impede the multicultural counseling process with interracial individuals.

I wrote this book to promote counselor awareness and interest in the needs and strengths of interracial people, to provide initial guidelines for counseling interracial people, and to help counselors see how much our profession has neglected this special population. I hope that this book will serve as a "springboard" to development of culturally sensitive counseling for individuals and families with more than one racial heritage.

ACKNOWLEDGMENTS

N umerous people lent support and assistance in the preparation of this manuscript. First, I extend my appreciation to those who read earlier drafts of the manuscript and provided insightful suggestions for revisions: Josephine Johnson (my colleague and friend of more than two decades who read the entire book), and Keren Humphrey and William McFarland (my colleagues who read drafts of various chapters). Rebecca Day, our departmental secretary, supervised student worker assistance with the tedious task of checking references. Next, I express special thanks to the many librarians at the Western Illinois University Library (especially those in the Government Documents, Reference, and Interlibrary Loan divisions) for their splendid assistance in locating relevant resources.

Joseph Ponterotto (Fordham University at Lincoln Center) and Jean Phinney (California State University, Los Angeles) provided assistance in contacting key people in the field of interracial counseling. Linda Line Alipuria graciously furnished a copy of her thesis.

Prepublication reviews by Christine Kerwin, Courtland Lee, and John McFadden have been helpful in finalizing the volume. To them I extend a sincere "thank you."

To my husband, Jim, I communicate the utmost gratitude for continuing to support me as a nontraditional wife, mother, grandmother, career woman, and retiree for more than four decades. His wide-ranging support (from resolving computer glitches to proofreading to expanding assistance with household duties) has been invaluable.

My special appreciation is extended to the ACA staff, particularly to Carolyn Baker, the Acquisitions and Development Editor, and Michael Comlish, the Managing Editor. Special thanks also to Annette Van Deusen, the Copy Editor, for her meticulous work. These people have helped me surmount earlier barriers to the completion of this book.

ABOUT THE AUTHOR

BEA WEHRLY, Ph.D., N.C.C., has 40 years of experience in teaching and counseling, the last 25 of which were as a counselor educator at Western Illinois University. She is the author of the 1995 Brooks/Cole book, *Pathways to Multicultural Counseling Competence: A Developmental Journey*, and serves as one of the editors of the *International Journal for the Advancement of Counseling*.

Wehrly developed and taught the multicultural counseling course at Western Illinois University for 8 years and has presented on multicultural topics at local, state, regional, national, and international conferences since 1980.

1

Interracial Individuals:

A Population in Need of Recognition by the Helping Services Field

"The emergence of a racially mixed population is transforming the 'face' of the United States" (Root, 1992d, p. 3). "Twenty-eight years after the last state anti-miscegenation law was struck down, an interracial generation is demanding its place at the American table" (Morganthau, 1995, p. 64). Both Root and Morganthau propose that the rapidly changing composition of the U.S. population may force us to reconsider what we believe about race and racial categories.

Since the early 1990s the popular press has seen an explosion of articles on the increasing interracial population in the United States (Aubrey, 1995; Bates, 1993; Begley, 1995; Cose, 1995; Courtney, 1995; Funder-

1

burg, 1994; Haizlip, 1994, 1995; Leslie, Elam, Samuels, & Senna, 1995; Mathabane & Mathabane, 1992; Morganthau, 1995; Perkins, 1994; Pressley, 1994; Updike, 1992; von Sternberg, 1995a, 1995b; Williams, 1995). In spite of the fact that there are large numbers of interracial individuals in the United States, there seems to have been a denial of their existence as a population with special needs and special strengths that deserve recognition by counselors.

Professionals in some of the social science fields have made the interracial population a target of considerable research; however, the helping services field has given scant attention to interracial individuals and families. In particular, there is a dearth of professional literature on interracial counseling. The purposes of this chapter are to introduce readers to the neglected interracial population and to present a rationale for counselor competency in work with interracial people.

One indication of the neglect of interracial individuals in the helping services field is the confusion that exists over the appropriate terminology to describe persons of more than one racial heritage. The terms *interracial* and *biracial* are currently found in the professional literature. Other descriptive terms used in the literature of previous decades are *multiracial, mixed, mulatto, brown, rainbow,* and *combination*. On occasion, the terms *bicultural* and *multicultural* are found. In recent years the meaning of the term *culture* has been broadened to include any kind of different population; therefore, use of the terms *bicultural* or *multicultural* do not accurately describe people with more than one racial heritage. I agree with Wardle (1987) in selecting the term *interracial* as the term of choice because it denotes individuals with two or more racial heritages. Because the terms *biracial, mixed race,* and *multiracial* are in common use by many authors, I will use these terms and *interracial* interchangeably in this book.

The section that follows includes discussion of forces that have created an urgency for counselors to recognize the unique needs and strengths of interracial individuals. It also highlights reasons why counselors may need to modify the counseling process to appropriately meet the unique qualities of interracial individuals and families.

Rationale for Counselor Competency in Work with the Interracial Population

Changing Forces in Society

In the past half century many social and cultural events have led to an increase in the number of interracial relationships and marriages (Davis, 1991; Gibbs, 1987, 1989; Kerwin & Ponterotto, 1995; McRoy & Freeman, 1986; Morganthau, 1995; Murphy-Shigematsu, 1987; Overmier, 1990; Root, 1992c; Thornton, 1992; Tucker & Mitchell-Kernan, 1990; Wardle, 1987). The 1954 Brown v. the Board of Education U.S. Supreme Court decision paved the path to the integration of public education, preschool through higher education. The 1967 Loving v. Virginia U.S. Supreme Court decision declared unconstitutional the miscegenation laws (laws against interracial marriage) that still existed in 16 states. These two Supreme Court decisions opened the legal doors for interracial relationships and interracial unions.

The heavy U.S. military presence in Asia since the onset of World War II led to U.S. military and civilian employees bringing spouses from Japan, Korea, the Philippines, Vietnam, Thailand, and other Asian countries to the United States for nearly a half century (Gibbs, 1989; Murphy-Shigematsu, 1987; Ranard & Gilzow, 1989; Thornton, 1992). Thousands of Amerasian children have been born to the approximately 80,000 American/Asian couples who have come to the United States since the early 1940s (Murphy-Shigematsu, 1987). The Amerasian Homecoming Act of 1987 allowed Vietnamese Amerasians (children of American servicemen stationed in Vietnam) and certain family members to be admitted to the United States as immigrants (U.S. Catholic Conference, 1988). Marcus, reporting in the March 8, 1992 *Washington Post*, noted that 14,000 Vietnamese Amerasians have come to the United States since the Homecoming Act of 1987.

The Civil Rights movement of the 1960s and 1970s, the counterculture movement of the 1960s and 1970s, and the Women's Movement of the 1970s and 1980s helped to lessen societal sanctions against interracial relationships and marriage (Brandell, 1988; Davis, 1991; Gibbs, 1987, 1989; Kalmijn, 1993; Leslie et al., 1995; Tucker & Mitchell-Kernan, 1990). These events led to racially mixed schools, neighborhoods, places of entertainment, and work settings. As interracial interactions increased in these settings, so have the number of interracial unions and interracial children from these unions. In 1987 Gibbs estimated that there were approximately one million interracial children in the United States. Estimates of the total U.S. interracial population are very difficult to obtain and will be discussed in the next section.

Demographic Changes

Accurate statistics on the numbers of interracial people in the United States are difficult to obtain largely because of the way in which U.S. census data are collected (Sandor, 1994). Respondents to the census questionnaires do not have the option of checking a category entitled "biracial," "interracial," or "mixed." On the census questionnaire, respondents are told to mark "ONE" category for the race they consider themselves to be. At the end of the possible choices there is an "Other race" box in which some respondents wrote in "multiracial," "multiethnic," "mixed," or "interracial" in the 1990 census; thus individuals are beginning to indicate that they have more than one racial heritage. This is not the same, however, as having the choice to state clearly one's interracial heritage.

The U.S. Bureau of the Census *Marital Status and Living Arrangements: March 1992* reports that the number of interracial couples involving one Black or one White spouse almost quadrupled between 1970 and 1992, increasing from 310,000 in 1970 to 1,161,000 in 1992. These numbers do not reflect the growing number of interracial couples who are dating or living together. The validity of demographic data on biracial children is influenced by the reluctance of people to give interracial identification on marriage applications and on children's birth certificates (Gibbs, 1989; Kerwin & Ponterotto, 1995).

Tucker and Mitchell-Kernan (1990) noted that "overall national interracial marriage rates are deceptive, disguising marital patterns that differ quite substantially on the basis of ethnicity, gender, and geographic location in particular" (p. 209). They report that interracial marriage for Japanese and for Native American women is practically normative with 40.6% of Japanese and 53.7% of Native American females in interracial marriages. African Americans are the only major racial ethnic group where male outmarriage (marriage with someone of another race) exceeds that of females. Rates of outmarriage for Black males are the lowest in the South and the highest in the West.

Tucker and Mitchell-Kernan's (1990) research sheds light on the correlates of Black interracial marriage in the West, the part of the United States that has the highest rates of Black outmarriage. It also shows the pressures that those involved in interracial marriage feel from their families and communities of origin. Persons living in the West who intermarried were likely to be born in a region where the attitudes toward interracial marriage were more permissive (the North) or where the person had not acquired firsthand knowledge of race relations in the United States (the foreign born). Rates of interracial marriage for people born in the West were no higher than for interracial marriage rates in the South. Blacks who intermarried were more inclined to live away from the community where they were born. The authors suggested that the interracial couple's tendency to move away from their place of birth was "a function of the enduring familial and community control over mate selection" (Tucker & Mitchell-Kernan, 1990, p. 214).

There are many more people in the United States who have a mixed racial heritage than the census data report (Cose, 1995). Root (1992d) asks the question, "Why has the United States suppressed the historical reality that a significant proportion of its citizenry has multigenerational roots?" (p. 7). Davis (1991) calls attention to the "unknown" mixed heritage of both Black and White Americans in his book, *Who Is Black?* Anthropologists and sociologists estimate that 75% to 90% of Black Americans have White ancestors and up to 25% of Black Americans have Native American ancestors. Lillian Smith (1961) addresses the issue of the fathering of biracial children by the White southern plantation owners. Davis (1991) states that at least 1% of White Americans have Black ancestors, whereas Haizlip (1994, 1995) suggests that the percentage of White Americans with Black ancestors is much higher than the 1% figure. In their popular book, *Having Our Say*, Delaney, Delaney, and Hearth (1993) discuss their mixed Black, White, and Native American racial roots.

Other individuals in the United States with mixed racial heritages are the people whose parents are of different persons of color heritage. Root (1992d) notes that the mixing of persons of color with other persons of color "—such as American Indians and Blacks, Filipinos and Native Americans, Latinos and Blacks—has been given little attention in the literature" (p. 6).

Paucity of Professional Literature on Work With Interracial Individuals and Families

Literature on cross-cultural and multicultural counseling has increased dramatically in the past two decades (Lee & Richardson, 1991; Ponterotto & Casas, 1991; Wehrly, 1991, 1995). However, work with people of biracial or interracial heritage has rarely been addressed in the multicultural counseling literature (Brandell, 1988; Gibbs, 1987; Herring, 1992; Overmier, 1990; Root, 1990; Wardle, 1987).

In reviewing tables of contents and indexes in recent textbooks on multicultural counseling, diversity, or both (Atkinson & Hackett, 1995; Atkinson, Morten, & Sue, 1993; Axelson, 1993; Baruth & Manning, 1991; Lee, 1995; Lee & Richardson, 1991; Locke, 1992; Pedersen, 1994; Pedersen, Draguns, Lonner, & Trimble, 1989; Ponterotto, Casas, Suzuki, & Alexander, 1995; Sue & Sue, 1990; Wehrly, 1995) references were found to "biracial" or "interracial" in the tables of contents or the indexes of 4 of the 12 books (Baruth & Manning, 1991; Pedersen et al., 1989; Ponterotto et al., 1995; and Wehrly, 1995). It would appear that interracial people continue to be a neglected population in the multicultural counseling literature.

Some literature on biracial/interracial people is available in social science professional journals. Professional counseling journals include very few articles devoted solely to work with biracial or interracial persons. I found that Black-White interracial issues are researched and addressed more commonly than issues of other interracial individuals (Brandell, 1988; Gibbs, 1987, 1989; Hill & Peltzer, 1982). Discussion of the role of a biracial/interracial adult as a parent is rarely found in the counseling literature.

Root (1990, 1992c) sees society's silence on biracialism as a source of oppression and suggests that society has acted as if the problem will go away if it is ignored. Poussaint (1984) notes that a factor contributing to the paucity of research on interracial families and children is that it is often difficult to get parents of interracial children to give their consent to interview any family members. In their 1992 book, the Mathabanes challenged interracial couples to speak out: "we mixed couples, if we ever want to be fully understood, accepted, and respected by society, have to be willing to tell our human stories in order to combat stereotypes about us; we have to speak out against bigotry, black and white, wherever we may live" (p. 190).

At a recent conference of over 300 Midwest human service workers, I asked the luncheon group how many have worked, or are working, with children of more than one racial heritage. Almost all the helping service people present raised their hands. Professionals have become cognizant of the increasing number of people of biracial/interracial heritage they are called upon to serve. One might assume that the dearth of professional literature to provide guidelines for meeting the unique needs of this population has hampered the delivery of appropriate services.

Persistence of Social Barriers

Although the U.S. public was introduced to Julie, a biracial Black-White leading lady, in the popular mid-20th century musical, *Showboat*, almost no recognition was given to societal racism and discrimination as a source of Julie's problems. It appears that the sheriff's statement, "One drop of Black blood makes you Black in these here parts," did little to help people understand the limits that this stereotype imposes on people of more than one racial heritage.

In her 1994 book, *Black, White, Other: Biracial Americans Talk about Race and Identity*, Funderburg discusses the paradox of the "one-drop rule." She points out that it is never a two-way street. "One can be black and have 'white blood' (even to the point of having a white parent . . .) but one cannot be white *and* have 'black blood' " (Funderburg, 1994, p. 13).

"No other ethnic population in the nation, including those with visibly non-caucasoid features, is defined and counted according to the one-drop rule" (Davis, 1991, p. 12). The one-drop rule was strongly supported by the Jim Crow system that was subscribed to for decades after the freeing of the slaves. Davis also calls attention to the fact that the one-drop rule and the anxiety experienced by Blacks who attempted to pass as Whites originated during slavery. Haizlip (1994) details the pain her mother experienced when her mother's siblings chose to flee, break all ties with their sister, and "pass" in the White world.

Current evidence of negative social barriers against interracial couples and children of interracial unions abounds. One such example came in early 1994 when an interracial Black-White teenager in Wedowee, Alabama, was told by her high school principal that her parents' marriage was "a mistake." The same school principal announced that the high school prom would be cancelled if interracial couples planned to attend (Pressley, 1994; Staff, 1994, September). Courtney (1995), a Black/White biracial student at the University of Tennessee, described how his life has been a neverending tug-of-war because of societal pressures to make him choose one side of his racial heritage over the other. Interracial couples still face stares and negative vibes when seen in public in many parts of the United States. A question that invariably is asked of interracial couples is "But what about the children?" (Funderburg, 1994; Pressley, 1994).

Some writers believe that interracial couples experience somewhat greater acceptance than in past decades (Gibbs, 1989; Sebring, 1985; Wardle, 1987). However, social barriers and racism still place added stressors on many interracial couples and their children (Brandell, 1988; Funderburg, 1994; Marcus, 1992; Mathabane & Mathabane, 1992; Overmier, 1990; Pressley, 1994; Root, 1990; Wardell, 1987). Mathabane and Mathabane (1992) note that "it is the black man— white woman combination that sparks the most widespread condemnation among both blacks and whites" (p. 255). The negative view of much of society toward interracial individuals, couples, and families persists.

The children of the union of a Black parent with a parent of any other race are still considered Black by the majority of people in the United States (as in the *Showboat* era). These children are not given the option to consider themselves biracial or interracial by most of society (Brandell, 1988; Davis, 1991; Funderburg, 1994; Lyles, Yancey, Grace, & Carter, 1985; Poussaint, 1984; Root, 1990, 1992c). Many children of other White/non-White unions are also identified by the race of the non-White parent. The White partner of an interracial union may have his or her first experience of being a target of racism when the couple "goes public" on their relationship. The birth of their first child often heightens the societal prejudices that the White parent feels over the public's reaction to this interracial baby. Mathabane and Mathabane (1992) state: "These trials of white partners in interracial relationships, though just as frustrating and dehumanizing as those experienced by the black partners, are seldom acknowledged" (p. 177).

Myths and Stereotypes

A number of myths and stereotypes about interracial individuals, couples, and families are omnipresent in the United States. The early myths of White superiority and supremacy and the dangers of racial mixing (miscegenation) and "mongrelization" that were supported by conservative thinking, individual interpretations of the Bible, or both are still believed by some people (Davis, 1991). It has been difficult to get beyond the "mongrelization" myth that the interracial child will inherit only negative traits of both parents.

Other myths relate to the motives of either or both partners for entering into an interracial relationship (Wardle, 1992a). Some people believe that marriage to someone of a different race is an attempt to "get back" at society or is a marriage for an ulterior motive. White partners, especially females, may be accused of "acting out" unresolved problems with their parents. Black partners may be accused of trying to "make it" and gain prestige. It is difficult for many people in society to believe that the partners in an interracial relationship can truly be attracted to each other on a positive, loving basis.

The automatic labeling of the child of a White/non-White union as a non-White, as discussed in the previous section, could be considered a myth. Other myths are that all White females entering into a relationship with Black males are whores and that females of interracial heritage are more exotic and more sexually attractive. The belief that partners in an interracial marriage are fugitives and outcasts from the real world is another pervasive myth.

One blatant myth is to view all problems of interracial individuals and families as race-related problems when, in fact, they may be normal or developmental issues faced by all people. Wardle (1992a) lists another myth as "Minorities are more accepting of biracial children than are non-minorities" (p. 165). And the list goes on. It is obvious that there is a great need for society to move beyond these pervasive myths and stereotypes and to see interracial people and people of color as full partners in the human race.

The myths cited persist as the result of stereotyping. Stereotypes are developed at a very early age and are influenced by the ongoing socialization process. Parents, family members, peers, and other agents of socialization contribute to the myths and stereotypes that all of us hold about interracial people. An interesting fact noted by Funderburg (1994) is that the number of interracial people in films, literature, entertainment, or the news is very small. However, the entertainment industry has begun to highlight interracial romances through TV series such as "LA Law" and "General Hospital," and through movies such as *Jungle Fever*, *The Joy Luck Club*, *The Bodyguard*, and *Mississippi Masala* (Perkins, 1994).

Summary

This chapter has introduced readers to a population that has been greatly neglected by the counseling profession. Several topics were addressed to provide a rationale for counselor attention to interracial individuals and to people in interracial relationships. The changing societal forces that have brought about the demographic increase in interracial unions and the birth of children of more than one racial heritage have been reviewed. The paucity of counseling literature that addresses the needs and the strengths of the interracial population was underscored. Myths and stereotypes about men and women who enter into interracial relationships and about people with more than one racial heritage were discussed.

Root (1992d, 1994) and Morganthau (1995) believe that the "face" of the United States is being transformed by the rapidly growing racially mixed population. "At some core level, the variability in the visual appearance of the mixed-race person challenges the meaning of race and the order of the world predicated on it" (Root, 1994, p. 458). This chapter has challenged counselors in the United States to meet the needs of the people of this changing "face."

2

Historic Perspectives on Interracial Identity Development

"An unresolved research question in a multiracial society is whether or not it is possible for a child to develop a truly interracial identity" (Vaughan, 1987, p. 89). "The integration of biracial heritage into a positive self-concept is complicated and lengthy. . . . It is the marginal status imposed by society rather than the objective mixed race of biracial individuals which poses a severe stress to positive identity development" (Root, 1990, pp. 186 & 188).

Vaughan and Root challenge readers to think about aspects of identity development of interracial individuals. The statements also reflect the impact of current societal prejudice toward people with more than one

13

racial heritage. Most interracial individuals face barriers to positive identity development. There is, however, recent research to repudiate the myth that all biracial/interracial people are marginal in status.

The purposes of this chapter are: (a) to introduce readers to the challenges that interracial individuals face in developing an ethnic identity and (b) to review historic perspectives on identity development of interracial individuals. Current perspectives on interracial identity development are discussed in the chapters that address counseling with interracial individuals at the various developmental levels (Chapters 4, 5, and 6).

Literature on identity development of interracial individuals is not abundant (Alipuria, 1990; Funderburg, 1994; Lyles et al., 1985; Poston, 1990; Root, 1990, 1992c). The existing literature on racial identity development of interracial individuals is limited because of several factors. Probably the most important factor is that biracial or interracial identity development was rarely addressed in the early literature because individuals who had more than one racial heritage were automatically identified under the category of their non-White heritage (when the interracial mix was White and non-White) (Root, 1990). If the interracial mix was of two people of color groups, the individual usually experienced oppression from the people of color group having the higher social status (Root, 1990). Choice in selecting a racial reference group identity was rarely given to the interracial individual.

A second factor influencing the paucity of professional literature on interracial individuals relates to the complexities of research with racially mixed people. Root (1992a, 1992b, 1992d) discusses past and present methodological issues in research with racially mixed people. The pros and cons of using qualitative, quantitative, and a rigorously applied combination of qualitative and quantitative research are delineated by Root (1992a).

Research on the development of racial/ethnic awareness in children is especially complex. We now know that some of the methodology used and conclusions drawn from early research of racial identity development of children of color and of interracial children were flawed (Aboud, 1987; Cross, 1991; Jacobs, 1977, 1992; Vaughan, 1987). Our awareness of the shortcomings of early racial identity development research of children led to discounting basic contributions of these early researchers (e.g., findings that children's attitudes about race are formed early in life and are developed in a complex manner).

Closely related to the complexities and challenges of research with racially mixed people in the United States is the reality that most current racial identity development models are inappropriate for describing the identity development process of people with more than one racial heritage (Hall, 1992; Herring, 1992, 1995; Jacobs, 1992; Kich, 1992; Miller, 1992; Poston, 1990; Reynolds & Pope, 1991; Root, 1990, 1992c). In recent years new models for studying the identity development of interracial adults have been presented (Kich, 1992; Poston, 1990; Reynolds & Pope, 1991; Root, 1990). Time is needed to conduct research on the efficacy of the new models for describing interracial identity development. We are currently at a point in time where there is a need for much work (both theory building and research) on how the interracial individual develops a racial identity. Root's rationale for using both qualitative and quantitative research can be helpful in designing these studies (Root, 1992a).

Several topics are addressed in the chapter sections that follow. First, historic perspectives on interracial individuals as well as historic perspectives on identity development models in general are presented. The chapter then addresses historic perspectives on interracial identity development for interracial children, adolescents, and adults. Early research on identity development of interracial people is cited as it applied to the various developmental levels. Because authors vary on the choice of terms used for the reference group identity of one's parental heritage, the terms *racial, cultural,* and *ethnic* are used interchangeably throughout this chapter and the rest of the book to indicate heritage.

Historic Perspectives on Interracial People and Identity Development Models

Alipuria (1990) states that there are three background areas to consider "before looking at empirical research on the multiracial population" (p. 11). This discussion of historic perspectives on interracial people and identity development models is organized under the three areas discussed by Alipuria (1990): Science and Race Mixing, Marginal Man, and the History of Race Mixing in the United States.

Science and Race Mixing

The first area reviewed by Alipuria, Science and Race Mixing, includes the evolution of viewpoints on the scientific view of race mixing. Changes reported by geneticists over the years are noted. Non-Whites were viewed as inferior when European settlers wished to justify colonialization and enslavement. Negative and dire results were predicted for the children of miscegenation. By the mid-1930s some new scientific evidence showed that human heredity was much more complex than originally thought. At this time people were also feeling "the need to repudiate the Nazi stand on race mixing" (Alipuria, 1990, p. 13). After World War II, the geneticists declared that race mixing was not detrimental and sometimes even favorable. However, public views on the mixing of races seem to have been minimally influenced by the post–World War II scientific reports.

Marginal Man

In the 1920s Robert Park wrote about the Marginal Man (Alipuria, 1990). Park described this person as a biracial individual between two cultures who had the potential for a broader perspective, a keener intelligence, and a more objective and rational view of the world. Everett Stonequist (1937) expanded on the concept of the marginal man developed by Robert Parks. Stonequist's 1937 book, *The Marginal Man: A Study in Personality and Culture Conflict*, presented an early 20th-century perspective on the Eurasians or Anglo-Indians of India, the Cape Coloured of South Africa, the Mulattoes of the United States, the Coloured People of Jamaica, the Indo-Europeans of Java, the Part Hawaiians, and the Metis of Brazil.

After discussing early 20th-century historic, economic, demographic, and sociopolitical factors that influenced each society's prevailing view of people of mixed racial heritage, Stonequist (1937) noted that the "racial hybrids" and "mixed bloods" were viewed as undesirable in India, South Africa, and the United States where race relations were most intense. "Because of his peculiarities the mixed blood presents a special problem to the community. . . . [and] will become the target of whatever hostile sentiments exist between the parent races" (Stonequist, 1937, p. 10). Stonequist (1937) questioned whether "the 'theories' about the characters of mixed bloods are merely rationalizations of existing practices and prejudices of a particular situation" (p. 49). He seemed to realize the powerful impact of societal racism on the mixed race individual; in general, however, Stonequist's descriptions reflected the ethnocentric viewpoints of the dominant White society in the United States of that era and that continue to influence attitudes of people in contemporary society.

Alipuria (1990) states that "the marginal man theory raises psychological questions for multiracial persons" (p. 15). Some of the issues raised by Alipuria are whether or not multiracial people are (a) more tolerant than their monoracial peers because of a wider vision or (b) more troubled because of their hypersensitivity and difficulties in finding a place to belong. Alipuria also wonders about the role of context in influencing how marginal a multiracial individual may feel.

History of Race Mixing in the United States

Detailed information on the history of race mixing in the United States is given by Alipuria (1990), Cose (1995), Davis (1991), and Spickard (1989). Race mixing in the United States began soon after the Europeans and African slaves came to the North American continent. Wilson (1992) provides a history of the race mixing of Native Americans with the Europeans and with the African slaves.

Spickard (1989) traces the history of mixed blood in the United States and delineates the paths of intermarriage for Japanese Americans, American men and Japanese women after World War II, Jewish Americans, and Black Americans. His in-depth treatment of the sociopolitical history of these four groups in the United States includes discussion of several theories of intermarriage (e.g., social and economic conditions that encourage intermarriage, size of the minority community and intermarriage, social class and intermarriage, social distance and intermarriage, and impact of the triple-melting pot). Spickard notes the importance of the interplay of societal cultures and structure and how this influences people's perceptions, attitudes, and behaviors. Some of the other issues discussed by Spickard are the intense pressures that intermarriages face from outside of the family and the ongoing societal concerns of what happens to children of intermarriage. He also recognizes that "one of the general trends of this century was a general lessening of ethnic tensions and ethnocentric harrassment of intermarrying people" (Spickard, 1989, p. 359).

The Euro-Western culture that has dominated the history of the United States has attempted to control the mixing of races for much of the time. When it became clear that it was impossible to control the mixing of races, a myth that the mixed-race person would disappear arose. The acceptance of mixed-race persons in the United States has varied also by geographic location. A more permissive attitude "was prevalent in areas settled by way of the West Indies plantation society influenced by Spanish and French culture" (Alipuria, 1990, p. 17). The mixed-race lighter-skinned mulatto people of the Creole communities in South Carolina and Louisiana had higher status than the "Negroes" in those areas. Race mixing continued as slave owners used their female slaves as mistresses.

Haizlip (1994) underscores the difficult times experienced by the 400,000 mulattoes of Black and White heritage following the Civil War. The country seemed to have a blind spot that these people existed, "a mass denial of the intimate relationships between the powerful majority and the impotent minority. . . . Negroes were especially conflicted about the living, breathing visible evidence of plantation owners' power. Shamed by their own helplessness, they could not divorce natural sympathy for the victims from anger at those who, after all, possessed the former oppressors' blood" (Haizlip, 1994, p. 56). Mulattoes were treated with scorn, were abused, or were ignored.

The result was that after the Civil War there was ruthless enforcement of societal restrictions on interracial mating and marriage. Lighter-skinned African Americans held higher status within their own racial group; but to White Americans, anyone with "one drop" of "Negro" blood was considered "Negro" by the dominant society. It was not until the societal events discussed in Chapter 1 (intermarriage of U.S. military and civilian personnel with foreign nationals since World War II, the Supreme Court decisions of 1954 and 1967, and the Civil Rights movement of the 1960s and 1970s), that interracial relationships and marriage have shown a notable increase. J. R. Washington's 1970 book, *Marriage in Black and White*, presents perspectives on cross-racial marriages from that era.

Historic Perspectives on Racial/Cultural/Ethnic Identity Development of Interracial Children

An early study of racial awareness in young children (Goodman, 1952) is worthy of mention here because the results called attention to one of the myths about young children's racial awareness. The results of Goodman's research with 103 4-year-olds in an urban area of the northeast United States dispelled the then-prevalent notion that children of this age pay no attention to race. A few of the children in the study were of mixed racial heritage. For the purposes of the research, the mixed-race children were classified as "Negro" (the term used for African Americans of that era). (Note how the "one drop" theory influenced the classification of these 4-year-olds!)

The Goodman researchers with the 57 "Negroes" and the 46 White children were startled to find how much attention these children gave to race. The researchers realized that this awareness was more than an intellectual awareness. They were shocked "to find that four-year-olds, particularly white ones, show unmistakable signs of the onset of racial bigotry" (Goodman, 1952, p. 218). "An equally grim corollary was that 'Negro' children not yet five can sense that they are marked and grow uneasy" (Goodman, 1952, p. 218).

From the results of their detailed case studies, the Goodman researchers concluded that race awareness begins early in life, proceeds gradually, and is a process that is much more complex than simply learning someone else's attitudes. In summarizing the process of race awareness in children, Goodman (1952) stated that "each individual *generates* his own attitudes, out of the personal, social, and cultural materials which happen to be his" (p. 219).

Vaughan (1987) reviewed late 19th- and early 20th-century views on ethnic identity and attitude development of children. During this time some writers believed that humans had an instinctive fear of strangers and an innate sense of race. The first studies of children's ethnic identity development were done in the 1930s and used line drawings. In the 1940s and 1950s dolls were introduced with several studies using pictures, dolls, or both to study children's ethnic and racial attitude development. Although the authors of these early studies did not define levels of ethnic awareness or agree on awareness between Black and White children, Vaughan (1987) gave these early researchers credit for "demonstrating that children's responses varied with age, that there was a developmental trend, and that race awareness was not developed fully at birth" (p. 75). These early researchers did *not* report on racial identity development of interracial children.

In 1968 Teicher reviewed societal attitudes of the 1950s and 1960s toward Negro-White couples and their interracial children. Three condensed case histories of the children of Negro-White families who had used the services of the Los Angeles County Hospital's Child Psychiatry Unit were presented by Teicher. Uppermost among the many problems presented by these interracial children were the challenges of racial identity development. A study in progress at the Los Angeles General Hospital at that time was addressing the impact of Negro-White marriages on their children's personality development, self-concept formation, and racial and sexual identification.

By the 1970s more researchers were beginning to study aspects of identity development in interracial children. In 1977, three doctoral candidates reported on various aspects of young children's racial identity development. The three 1977 doctoral dissertations and their authors were (a) *Skin Color Recognition, Preference and Identification in Interracial Children: A Comparative Study* by Wayne Gunthorpe; (b) *Black/White Interracial Families: Marital Process and Identity Development in Young Children* by James Jacobs; and (c) *Racial Attitude Formation in Children of Mixed Black and White Heritage: Skin Color and Racial Identity* by Ruth Payne. All three of the investigators noted the shortcomings of previous studies of young interracial children.

Gunthorpe (1977) investigated skin tone recognition, preference, and identification in twenty-five 3-, 4-, and 5-year-old interracial children of Black and White parents and compared these results with matched pairs of Black children and White children of the same age. All of the children were able to recognize racial skin color differences. None of the children in the three groups showed clearly defined skin color preferences. The one difference that emerged in the results of Gunthorpe's study was that the majority of Black children were inaccurate in their skin tone identification whereas the majority of the White and interracial children could accurately identify their skin tone. Gunthorpe suggested that this high level of misidentification by Black children might result from poor self-esteem. Overall he found little evidence of strong ethnocentrism among the White children and little evidence of rejection of their own group by the Black children.

Jacobs (1977) reported on a study of seven intact Black-White families of middle-class status. He proposed two distinctly different stages in the identity development of these 3- to 8-year-old Black/White interracial children. In the first stage, children have not yet developed the cognitive concept of color constancy and are not able to classify dolls or pictures into racial groups by color of skin. At about 4½ years of age the child moves into the second stage and can attain color constancy and internalize an interracial label, providing that the parents have introduced the interracial label to the child. Jacobs (1977) found four qualities of parenting as "supportive of positive interracial self-concept formation: 1) early ego enhancing treatment, 2) providing an interracial label for the child, 3) assistance in verbalizing racial material and supportive interest in expression of racial ambivalence, and 4) multiracial associations" (p. 5023-B).

Jacobs continued to research the identity development of interracial children and published an updated version of his model in 1992. This revised model of identity development in biracial children (Jacobs, 1992) will be delineated in Chapter 4 in the section entitled Jacobs' Revised Model.

Payne (1977) researched the effects of race of parents, as well as the skin color, age, and sex of the child on 10 questions covering five areas of racial attitude formation. Payne studied eighty-one 2- to 6-year-old children of mixed Black and White heritage, of Black heritage, and of White heritage. She found differences in the way mixed-race children and Black or White children responded in the areas of racial identification and preference. Single-race children selected the darker dolls as not pretty more often than the mixed-race children. Mixed-race children most often selected dolls whose skin tone was closest to their own as the dolls that were not pretty. There were no differences among the groups in racial awareness. The mixed-race children's racial identity choices seemed to be influenced most by their own skin color and next by the race of their mothers.

Payne's research supported previous findings indicating that children are able to differentiate skin color by 3 years of age and begin to evidence preferences for skin color and physical attractiveness at an early age. Payne felt that the results of her research pointed to the critical importance of racial attitude development in the preschool years.

Historic Perspectives on Racial/Cultural/Ethnic Identity Development of Interracial Adolescents

Erik Erikson's early theories of identity development as presented in his books, *Childhood and Society* (1950, 1963), *Identity: Youth and Crisis* (1968), and *Identity and the Life Cycle* (1980) have had a major impact on perspectives on adolescent identity development. Erikson believed that the development of the adolescent's self-concept took place primarily through interacting with others.

Perhaps Erikson is remembered most for his concepts on the importance of the attainment of a stable identity during adolescence. Erikson (1968) was one of the first to define three types of identities for the individual: (a) ego identity, (b) personal identity, and (c) group identity. Ego identity relates to the individual's awareness of being a unique person. Personal identity involves the individual's perception that his or her personality has a sameness and continuity and that others also are aware of this sameness. Group identity is how the individual connects or relates to the context of the primary group in which the person lives and interacts.

Although Erikson did not address the identity development issues of interracial youth directly, much of what he has written about the negative impact of White racism on youth of color applies to interracial young people. In the second edition of *Childhood and Society* (1963), Erikson warned of the devastating effect of White racism on the identity development of youth whose skin color or culture were different.

An entire chapter, "Race and the Wider Identity," was included in *Identity: Youth and Crisis* (Erikson, 1968). The young person of color was seen as searching for an answer to the question, "Who am I?" Erikson felt that an even greater issue faced by the young person of color was how this person would perceive his or her opportunities in life, given the parameters of White racism on non-White individuals.

Gibbs (1987, 1989) refers to Erikson's model in her writings and discusses challenges faced by the biracial adolescent in attaining the stable identity listed by Erikson as the central developmental task of the adolescent. Additional information on Gibbs's perspectives on the racial and ethnic identity development of biracial adolescents is included in Chapter 5 in the section entitled Contemporary Perspectives on the Racial/Cultural/Ethnic Identity Development of Interracial Adolescents.

In 1966 James Marcia published an adolescent ego identity development model that extended the work of Erik Erikson. Marcia's 1980 revision of the model proposed four ego identity stages: identity achievement, foreclosure, identity diffusion, and moratorium. The concepts of both Erikson and Marcia are integrated into Jean Phinney's model of adolescent ethnic identity development (1989, 1993). Phinney's model is appropriate for use with interracial adolescents and will be discussed in Chapter 5 in the section Contemporary Perspectives on the Racial/Cultural/Ethnic Identity Development of Interracial Adolescents.

Historic Perspectives on the Racial/Cultural/Ethnic Identity Development of Interracial Adults

The earlier perspectives on the marginal status of people with more than one racial/cultural/ethnic heritage have been pervasive and long lasting. These viewpoints have been reviewed in the section Historic

Perspectives on Interracial People and Identity Development Models in this chapter. Research on the ethnic identity development of interracial adults is of relatively recent origin. Since the 1980s several dissertations have reported on studies of biracial adults. These empirical research reports have added perspectives on racial identity development in adults of more than one racial heritage. Details of the findings of these research reports are included in Chapter 6 in the section Contemporary Perspectives on Racial/Cultural/Ethnic Identity Development of Interracial Adults.

Clinical Case of an Interracial Adult

Historically, there has been scant reference in the counseling psychology literature to therapy with biracial/interracial individuals. A case study describing the challenges a biracial man faced in developing an integrated identity during the 1920s and 1930s was presented by Vita Sommers (1964). Sommers described the identity confusion and self-hatred experienced by the son of a southern Black mother and a Puerto Rican father. Because miscegenation laws prevented his parents from marrying, this individual carried his mother's name. For the first 7 years of his life, the boy developed a close relationship with his father. The young man was devastated when his father left the family and they were forced to move to an all-Black neighborhood where his peers jeered at him and terrorized him with threats. Sommers stated that the two factors leading to the extreme picture of conflict and self-hatred presented by this biracial individual were the agonizing separation from his father and the brutal treatment he received from society.

Summary

This chapter has introduced readers to the challenges that interracial individuals face in developing an ethnic identity. Historic perspectives on racial/cultural/ethnic identity development of interracial individuals were presented. A developmental perspective was taken in discussing the historic perspectives on the racial/cultural/ethnic identity development of children, adolescents, and adults.

3

Introduction to Counseling Interracial Individuals and Families

ll counseling with interracial individuals is cross-cultural unless the counselor is of the same interracial heritage as the counselee. Because an identical counselor-client interracial heritage combination will be rare in contemporary society, the counselor will need to keep in mind the content outlined in this chapter.

The purpose of this chapter is to review and apprise readers of general considerations that may apply in the process of counseling with an interracial person or family member of any age. Many of the topics to be discussed are taken from guidelines for cross-cultural or multicultural counseling. (See Appendix A, Proposed Cross-Cultural Competencies and Objectives, by Sue,

Arredondo, & McDavis, 1992.) The process guidelines presented in this chapter are tailored for application in working with interracial individuals.

This chapter focuses on two major aspects of the process of counseling with interracial individuals or families. First, the focus is on the counselor as a coworker with interracial individuals; second, the focus is on general guidelines for the process of counseling with interracial individuals or families. Succeeding chapters in this book address work with interracial children, adolescents and young adults, adults, and families.

The Counselor in a Working Relationship with an Interracial Individual or Family

The counselor who works with interracial individuals and families will need to have developed a firm sense of her or his own ethnic or racial identity. Hoare (1991) develops a strong case for the teacher or counselor who works with those who are culturally different to "first have a firm sense of self before he or she can move to an inclusive and relational identity" (pp. 51–52). For counselors to be able to accept others who are different, they need to feel good about their own racial/ethnic cultural heritages.

Counselor Self-Study of Ethnic/Racial Heritage

Developing a firm sense of one's own racial/ethnic identity is especially important for White counselors because people who are White frequently do not think of themselves as having a racial identity (Helms, 1984, 1990, 1992; Ponterotto & Pedersen, 1993; Rotheram & Phinney, 1987; Wehrly, 1991, 1995). Having knowledge of one's racial and ethnic history value systems is an important initial step in development of this firm sense of reference group identity.

The process of self-study of one's ethnic and racial heritage is described in detail in Wehrly (1995). Briefly, some of the types of information needed are the following. For people whose ancestors came from other countries, it is important to look into the reasons why the ancestors came to North America. Consideration needs to be given, also, to when the ancestors came to this part of the world, how their ethnic group was treated by the people already here, and the traditional values of this racial/ethnic group. For the original residents of North America, the Native Americans or the First Nation people, it is important to study the history of the treatment of this group by the European immigrants who came and took the land that was occupied by the Native American or First Nation people.

An additional component of one's ethnicity is to review contemporary values held by the groups that represent one's heritage. Counselors will need to take a hard look at how they have been influenced by the values of their heritages. This will include examining current behavior that may be affected by these values.

After counselors have determined which racial and ethnic values guide their current behavior, an additional examination of the impact of the values of their heritages regarding interracial people will be important (Gibbs, 1989; Kerf-Wellington, 1992; Logan, Freeman, & McRoy, 1987; McRoy & Freeman, 1986; Poston, 1990; Sebring, 1985). This will include engaging in a thorough self-examination of personal values, biases, beliefs, feelings, and attitudes toward such topics as interracial dating, interracial couples, interracial unions, and children of interracial unions.

This self-examination is important in light of McRoy and Freeman's (1986) observations that social workers who had not engaged in close examination of their biases toward interracial children exhibited these biases through one of two responses. One response was to overemphasize the child's racial background. The other response was to deny that the child's racial heritage had anything to do with the child's behavior. Neither of these responses are productive. Brown (1987) also wrote of the necessity of helper self-examination of her or his own individual racism: "Workers must analyze and understand their own feelings toward such unions before they can work with black-white couples" (p. 26).

Counselors need to review "scripts" that they may carry from comments they heard from significant others when they were young. What did they hear as children or adolescents about interracial dating and about interracial marriages? What stereotypes or myths come to mind when they think about interracial people? What is the source of these stereotypes and myths? To how many of these myths does the counselor still subscribe? Does the counselor feel an urgency to stare at interracial individuals or to ask questions about the racial heritage of an individual who looks different? Has the counselor examined the source of this need to stare or ask questions? The most important question for the counselor to ask in this self-examination is whether or not, and how, one is acting on these biases, myths, or stereotypes.

At the conclusion of this study, it is hoped that the counselor has a firm sense of his or her racial and ethnic heritage. Along with this firm sense of one's heritage should come pride in the heritage as well as the awareness of some values that the counselor may need to change in order to be effective in cross-cultural counseling with interracial people.

Counselors who have recognized that they have been influenced by negative interracial scripts from childhood have taken a major step in preparing to work with interracial people or families. It may be a lifelong vigilant endeavor for counselors to monitor if and how they act on these negative scripts in work with people of more than one racial heritage.

Counselor Awareness of Guilt Related to Behavior of Majority People Toward People of Color

In-depth study of one's racial and ethnic heritage sometimes leaves the White counselor with feelings of guilt. Pinderhughes (1989) helps us understand the immobilizing effect that guilt can have on the majority White counselor. "Guilt can create a sense of powerlessness, demoralization, and poor self-esteem, driving people to atone by seeking punishment—even from those over whom they have had advantage" (Pinderhughes, 1989, p. 99). It is critical for counselors to be open to themselves and to recognize the impact that their race has had upon them. Since guilt can have such a negative effect on self-esteem, counselors may need to seek counseling to work through these feelings of guilt.

Guilt is sometimes a response to recognition of the power that one has by virtue of such factors as race, sex, social class, or ordinal position in one's family. Pinderhughes (1989) warns of the need for the clinician to carefully manage guilt and power in cross-cultural work.

Counselor Awareness of Societal Perspectives and Behaviors Toward Interracial People

Additional information that the counselor needs is an awareness of the way that many people in contemporary society continue to give negative messages to interracial individuals. One way for counselors to increase their knowledge of contemporary societal behavior toward, and the impact of this behavior on, interracial individuals and families is to read books such as: *Black, White, Other: Biracial Americans Talk About Race and Identity* by Lise Funderburg (1994); *Gift Children: A Story of Race, Family, and Adoption in a Divided America* by J. Douglas Bates (1993); *Life on the Color Line. The True Story of a White Boy Who Discovered He Was Black* by Gregory Howard Williams (1995); *Love in Black and White: The Triumph of Love Over Prejudice and Taboo* by Mark and Gail Mathabane (1992); *Multiracial Couples: Black and White Voices* by Paul C. Rosenblatt, Terri A. Karis, and Richard D. Powell (1995); and *The Sweeter the Juice* by Shirlee Taylor Haizlip (1994).

Counselor Awareness of the Impact of Culture on Racial/Ethnic Identity Development

Counselors may also need to review other aspects of cultural, racial, or ethnic identity development. The previous chapter included historic perspectives on the identity development of interracial individuals. It may be important, also, to review some basic concepts about the meaning of racial/ethnic identity.

"Identity is constructed from within the person and culture in which it is forged" (Hoare, 1991, p. 48). This identity is shaped in childhood and in adolescence and continues to be influenced in adulthood. The process of cultural identity development determines what each of us sees as reality in our own lives and provides us with what some people call *cultural lenses*. We wear these cultural lenses throughout our lifetime. None of us can totally escape the impact of our cultural, racial, or ethnic heritage reality (our cultural lenses) to be completely objective in understanding the reality of another. Hoare (1991) emphasizes this when she asks: "How can persons have culturally rooted identities, so important to maintenance of their values and ways of knowing, and yet be completely open to others?" (p. 52). If we can never be totally objective in understanding a person who has a single racial or ethnic heritage, maintaining objectivity can be increasingly challenging in work with an individual with more than one racial or ethnic heritage.

The Western concept of identity development stresses affiliating with persons and groups who are like self and repudiating persons and groups who are different from self. Carried to its fullest, this notion supports prejudice against those who are different (Hoare, 1991). Consider what repudiating those who are different could mean to an interracial individual.

Many of the 46 biracial individuals interviewed by Funderburg (1994) spoke of the dilemmas and struggles that they experienced in being pressured to choose to identify with only one of their racial heritages. The heart-rending process of repudiating part of self is described by one biracial individual this way:

> I identified black from childhood, and I never felt that I got any benefit from my mother's culture, her white heritage. I felt that I was denied something, denied a part of myself, because I never really quite fit in. (Funderburg, 1994, p. 374)

Hating or rejecting part of self is not viewed as a healthy resolution of building a positive identity for interracial people. This painful dilemma will be discussed more fully in each of the chapters that follow in this book.

Counselor Work With the Interracial Individual or Family in Counseling—Some Process Guidelines

Clinicians and researchers are beginning to furnish guidelines for counseling with interracial individuals. Lyles et al. (1985) suggest that major goals for counseling interracial individuals are to help them develop a greater sense of their racial roots as well as to help them develop pride in all parts of their racial heritage.

This chapter section is a compilation of general guidelines from the literature as well as guidelines that I have extrapolated from clinical and academic observations. Many of these guidelines address the Lyles et al. (1985) goals for counseling interracial individuals listed in the previous paragraph. The order of presentation of these guidelines does not imply that the item under discussion is more or less important than other topics discussed.

Learning About the Cultures of the Interracial Client

After counselor self-study and examination of her or his own racial and ethnic heritage, the counselor will find it helpful to engage in study of the various racial, ethnic, and cultural heritages of the interracial individual(s) with whom she or he is working. A detailed study of the process of learning about people of other cultures is given in Wehrly (1995). This process includes study of the historic and sociopolitical backgrounds of people of these cultures. It is particularly important for the counselor to be aware of the way the group (or groups) under study have been treated by the people of the majority culture.

At present there is a dearth of information on the historic and sociopolitical backgrounds of interracial people. This means that the study of the heritages of interracial individuals may need to be conducted one culture at a time.

Studying the traditional and current values of other cultures is also valuable preparation for cross-cultural counseling. This study is *not* for the purpose of stereotyping people from these cultural heritages. Knowledge of the sociopolitical history and values of cultural groups can assist the counselor in delivering more culturally sensitive service. In looking for information on traditional and current values of interracial people, the counselor will find very little literature on this topic. Again, it will probably be necessary to conduct separate investigations of traditional and current values held by people from each of the heritages of the interracial person.

It is always important to find out if the individual coming for help, the client, "owns" the values of his or her cultural roots. In the case of the interracial individual, this can lead to considerable exploration of the cultural heritages of that person. Exploring both, or all, racial heritages of the interracial client is critical (Gibbs, 1987).

Clients who have not explored both, or all, of their racial heritages may need help with this study. The model used by the counselor to study other races and cultures can be taught to the interracial client. At times, the counselor and client may be working together on this investigation.

Developing a Cross-Cultural Counseling Relationship With an Interracial Client

Developing a cross-cultural counseling relationship can be challenging when both counselor and counselee each have a single racial heritage. The challenge may be magnified when the counselor works with an individual with more than one racial heritage.

Gibbs (1985) details the development of a cross-cultural, Black-White working relationship for social workers. She delineates the importance of the interpersonal factors between the social worker and the client during relationship building. Wehrly (1995) has adapted Gibbs's relationship-building guidelines for cross-cultural counseling. Cross-cultural relationship building is a process that may occur in several stages and is especially appropriate for counseling with adolescents and adults. The process is reviewed here because it is applicable to counselor work with interracial counselees. Gibbs (1985) and Wehrly (1995) describe these four stages in cross-cultural relationship building:

Stage One is called the *Appraisal Stage*. At this time, there may be an extended period of "checking out" the counselor to see if that person can be trusted. The client is attempting to learn about the personal authenticity of the counselor (Gibbs, 1985).

In Stage Two, the *Investigative Stage*, the client may ask many questions to determine the counselor's value system and previous cross-cultural counseling experiences. Gibbs states that the key element here is egalitarianism. The client is determining if the counselor can relate as an equal. It is important for the interracial client to feel that the counselor accepts both or all of his or her racial heritages.

Stage Three, the *Involvement Stage*, is reached only if the client has felt positively about the interaction with the counselor in the first two stages. If the client reaches Stage Three, she or he will work to build a more personal relationship with the counselor and may invite the counselor to community or family ethnic events. The counselor is being tested as to whether he or she can operate within the cultural milieu of the counselee. Such invitations may require serious consideration so the counselor does not find himself or herself in a dual relationship with the counselee (Herlihy & Corey, 1992). At times, the counselor may need to explain professional ethics in declining some invitations. Otherwise, the client may feel rejected and refuse to come for more counseling.

If the counselor has passed the tests of the first three stages and is able to establish a more personal relationship with the counselee, the relationship moves to Stage Four, the *Commitment Stage*. The counselee feels that the counselor can accept him or her as an individual whose racial heritages are important. The counselor has shown a willingness to come to the cultural milieu (or milieus) of the client and understands the sociopolitical forces that operate in these cultural milieus.

The last stage, the *Engagement Stage*, is reached when the client becomes an active partner in the counseling process. The counselor has used interpersonal skills to engage the client. The client recognizes that this is an individual with whom he or she can work. At this point the professional skills of the counselor are the most important factor in the counseling process.

Gibbs (1985) reminds helping service personnel that this process may take more than one session. Counselors need to be sensitive to the importance of interpersonal skills in building a cross-cultural relationship so that interracial clients will reach the working stages (*Commitment* and *Engagement*) in counseling. Disregard for the importance of the relationship may lead to premature termination by the client.

Capitalize on Strengths and Advantages of Being Interracial

Once a solid relationship is built with interracial clients, it is usually appropriate to elicit their perspectives on the strengths or advantages of having more than one racial heritage. If a client can name no advantages, this may indicate negative feelings about being interracial. It could also mean that the client has not explored this issue.

Another avenue to explore is to see how the interracial client responds to findings of people who have asked this question of other interracial individuals. Hall (1992) noted several frequently mentioned positive comments from individuals who had dual heritages: being able to take the best qualities from both races; having a broader understanding of and ability to accept and empathize with people of other racial backgrounds; and gaining strength and positive life perspectives from being biracial. The 37 interracial individuals in Poussaint's 1984 report named these advantages of being biracial: (a) having parents from different racial heritages helped them to be more objective and have less bias toward certain groups of people; (b) being biracial meant they could move freely in the worlds of both of their parents and make many different kinds of friends, (c) having a White parent helped them feel less intimidated by the White world; and (d) being biracial sometimes led to a kind of favoritism.

The following quotes from interviewees in *Black, White, Other* (Funderburg, 1994) state advantages similarly: "being biracial has made me a stronger person and has kind of given me my own special gold card because I can understand black culture and white culture" (p. 49); "with two cultures you have your way into this and you have your way into that, you get to have all these great experiences because you get introduced to so many different things" (p. 327); "I'm proud to be mulatto" (p. 333). Capitalizing on and helping interracial clients see their strengths can help the clients build self-esteem.

Application of Racial/Ethnic Identity Development Models to the Interracial Individual's Struggle for Attainment of an Achieved Racial Identity

Although most of contemporary models for racial and ethnic identity development of interracial people are limited in their application to people of interracial heritage, it is still important for counselors to be aware of the general concepts from these models. Racial/ethnic identity models describe stages that people experience in attaining an achieved reference group identity. The process of attaining this feeling of confidence and pride in one's racial and ethnic heritage(s) can be painful. The interracial individual struggling to reach an achieved identity may experience negative emotions in this process.

Many authors of racial identity development models describe stages in which the individual may feel much anger toward others, even toward those of one's own heritage, as well as toward self (e.g., Helms, 1984, 1985, 1990, 1992; Kim, 1981; Ponterotto, 1988; Ruiz, 1990). Feeling anger may be part of the counselee's process of attaining a stable racial/ethnic identity. Counselors who feel defensive when counselees verbalize anger may need to examine the source of these feelings of defensiveness and consider how they can respond appropriately to this anger.

Phinney's research (Phinney, 1989, 1992; Phinney & Alipuria, 1990; Phinney & Chavira, 1992; Phinney & Tarver, 1988) found that adolescents did not necessarily experience anger in the process of attaining an achieved identity. Her subjects did include some adolescents with mixed racial heritage. It may be that the younger age of the people in this study is one reason that anger was not evident in the process. Or it may be that these adolescents are being raised in an era and geographic location where societal pressures are different.

Regardless of the source of the anger of the counselee, the counselor needs to be prepared for a variety of negative counselee emotions. The counseling session can be a safe place for the interracial client to express feelings of anger and alienation (Poston, 1990). It may help the interracial client if the counselor tells him or her that feelings like anger and ambivalence are normal in working to attain an achieved interracial identity. Counselor interventions can focus on helping the client explore negative feelings and appropriate ways to *act on* negative feelings. Counselors working with adolescent clients whose anger has led to violence may find the Options to Anger program described by Crumbley, Aarons, and Fraser (1995) helpful in assisting these young people to understand their own anger and to develop tools to deal with the emotional and physical aspects of anger.

Do Not Assume All Problems Brought by Interracial Individuals Are Related to Their Interracial Heritages

A very important guideline for work with interracial people is not to assume that all problems brought by the individual are related to that person's interracial heritage (Gibbs, 1987, 1989; Winn & Priest, 1993). Interracial individuals rarely mention their racial heritage as the most important presenting problem in the initial interview (Brandell, 1988; McRoy & Freeman, 1986). Likewise, referrals of interracial people are usually made because of some type of behavior that is viewed as maladaptive by the person or agency making the referral.

As in all counseling, it is important to determine how the interracial client views her or his reason(s) for coming for counseling. The counselor also needs to ascertain the client's expectations for the counseling process. Following this, it is appropriate for the counselor to respond whether or not he or she anticipates being able to meet the client's expectations and goals.

After interracial clients reach the Commitment and Engagement counseling stage, these clients may share problems that they see as related to their mixed racial status. A challenge to the counselor at this time may be to help these clients separate normal developmental or life problems from issues associated with interracial status.

Bibliotherapy/Bibliocounseling as a Tool for Use With Interracial Individuals

One tool or technique that may be useful in work with interracial individuals of any age is bibliotherapy (sometimes called bibliocounseling). Bibliotherapy is the use of stories and novels for therapeutic purposes. In more simple terms bibliotherapy is "the use of books to help people" (Cornett & Cornett, 1980, p. 8). Bibliotherapy can be experienced through listening to, reading, or seeing the story acted out on stage or in a video or movie.

Some general principles and guidelines apply to the use of stories and books for therapeutic purposes. The use of bibliotherapy assumes that a human problem exists now or in the future, that the reader or listener will become personally involved with the characters or situations in the story, and that the reader or listener may gain insight on alternatives for solving present or future problematic situations (Cornett & Cornett, 1980; Wehrly, 1995).

Stories used for bibliotherapeutic experiences must be real and believable; fairy tales are inappropriate. The process of bibliotherapy includes three stages: identification, catharsis, and insight (Cornett & Cornett, 1980). In order for the reader, listener, or viewer to have a complete therapeutic experience, that person must be able to identify with one of the lead characters in the story. The person who can identify with the individual in the story will experience feelings of relief or catharsis, a purge of emotions, in learning that others also face and work out these problems. Following catharsis, the individual is able to integrate mind and emotions and identify possible solutions to problems.

Cornett and Cornett (1980) list four possible benefits that individuals involved in bibliotherapy may receive:

1. Through learning about people in situations similar to their own, readers, listeners, or viewers have vicarious experiences. Because the situation is happening to someone else, that situation is safe and poses little threat to the reader, listener, or viewer.
2. Through learning that others experience problems similar to their own, the readers, viewers, or listeners realize that they are not alone and that others face similar life challenges.
3. Readers, listeners, or viewers learn of the various ways that the main characters in the novels solve problems or work out situations that are similar to problems they are facing. In this way, individuals learn that there may be several alternatives for dealing with problems.
4. Descriptions of the way others work at solving problems can help people to engage in critical thinking.

Bibliotherapy with interracial individuals will need to be applied in an age-appropriate and situation-specific manner. The reading level must also be appropriate when counselees are expected to read their own books. In using bibliotherapy with any developmental level, the needs of the individual are taken into consideration, stories are selected to meet the individual's needs, and plans are made for an appropriate time and manner in which to use the story and to provide follow-up.

Chapters 4 through 7 include sections describing uses of stories and books about interracial people with preschool and elementary children, adolescents, adults, and families. Appendix B lists several novels and books that might meet bibliotherapeutic needs of inter-racial individuals and families. The books in Appendix B are listed by recommended age level of the reader or listener.

Other Guidelines for Counselor Work With Interracial Individuals

As noted earlier in this book, many people in our contemporary world will label the individual who is both Black and White as Black (Funderburg, 1994; McRoy & Freeman, 1986; Poussaint, 1984). Individuals of other White/non-White biracial heritage may find that they are identified by their non-White racial heritage. In cases where the racial heritage mix is of more than one non-White heritage, the individual may be seen as belonging to the race that is most different from the White race. This may be an area of frustration to explore in counseling with these biracial individuals.

In work with interracial children and adolescents, it is usually helpful to engage the other members of the family in counseling. Working with other family members as well as with the child or adolescent helps the young person to not feel stigmatized or singled out as the source of the problem (Gibbs, 1987, 1989; Lyles et al., 1985; McRoy & Freeman, 1986). Including other family members in counseling also helps the counselor assess the family support system of the client.

Listen for *loneliness* in work with interracial individuals. Feelings of not really belonging anywhere and feeling lonely were evident in many of the 46 interviews included in *Black, White, Other* (Funderburg, 1994). One biracial interviewee explained this feeling thus:

> When I was young, the way I saw myself was: I'm not *that*, and I'm not *that*, either. . . . I was both in a certain way, but in another way I was neither and I probably still largely think the same. (Funderburg, 1994, p. 264)

Another biracial Black/White interviewee talked about always being an outsider and not fitting anywhere:

> I was in these advanced-placement classes and I talked to the white students who were in the class, but they weren't good friends. I was recognized by the black community as an outstanding black student, of course. That used to upset me, that they would claim me because I did well academically, but I wasn't a part of their world. (Funderburg, 1994, p. 353)

Loneliness can begin very early in a child's life. Young children can sometimes be very cruel in the way they treat peers who are different.

Confusion over one's racial or ethnic identity is common among interracial people. Sorting out the perplexities with which the counselee is living may help. Gibbs (1987) states that the counselor may find a link between identity confusion and confusion in other areas with the interracial counselee.

Listen for possible themes of *victimization* in work with interracial individuals. When people feel powerless they sometimes take on the role of victim. Those biracial Black/White people who have strong identifications with their Black heritage may be struggling with not being caught in the victim status.

Steele (1990) writes how he was caught up in the Black victim identity movement:

> The civil rights movement and the more radical splinter groups of the late sixties were all dedicated to ending racial victimization, and the form of black identity that emerged to facilitate this made blackness and victimization virtually synonymous. . . . victimization became the overriding focus of racial identity. (p. 101)

Steele describes how clinging to this negative victim status serves as a barrier for individual development. He challenges African Americans to develop a collective identity that encourages diversity within the race, that does not make black unity a form of repression, that does not imply that the least among us are the most black, and that makes the highest challenge of "blackness" personal development. (Steele, 1990, p. 173)

The victim role may be played out in various ways. One manifestation of victimization is learned helplessness. Clients who are into learned helplessness are sometimes very manipulative (one way they can gain power in a situation). The counselor who works with people who act as victims may find self being manipulated by these clients. Counselors may need to address this manipulation "in the here and now" of counseling sessions and help these interracial clients realize the self-defeating behavior in which they are engaging.

Anger may be associated with feelings of victimization. Crumbley et al. (1995) write about anger and the victim role: "Most discussions of anger are really about the sense of victimization that justifies anger" (p. 4). Challenging victim thinking is one of the first steps in the Options to Anger program directed by these authors/practitioners.

The Role of Interracial Support Groups

In several areas of the United States support groups have been organized for interracial individuals and families. One of the interviewees in *Black, White, Other* (Funderburg, 1994) told how he was eager to associate with more people like himself and how he would like to see more functions for interracial people. Reports on these groups indicate that to date most of them are for college students, adults, and families. There is the potential to organize these groups for younger interracial individuals.

Counselors can explore their geographic areas to learn about support groups for their interracial clients. If none are in existence, perhaps counselors can help in organizing such support groups. More details on some of the interracial groups in existence are included in succeeding chapters.

Summary

This chapter has introduced general guidelines for counseling with interracial individuals and families. The first part of the chapter outlined several steps that the counselor can take to prepare for cross-cultural counseling with interracial clients. The last part of the chapter reviewed process guidelines for counseling with people with more than one racial heritage.

4

Counseling Preschool and Elementary Interracial Children

This chapter focuses on the process and content of counseling preschool and elementary interracial children. The effective child counselor will work not only with children, but also with the adults who are significant in the lives of these children.

Topics to be discussed in this chapter are: Counselor Self-Awareness as the First Step in Counseling Preschool and Elementary Interracial Children and Their Families, Issues Faced by Many Interracial Children, Contemporary Perspectives on the Racial/Cultural/Ethnic Identity of the Interracial Child, Counselor Roles in Work With Preschool and Elementary Interracial Children, and Special Considerations for Counseling Interracial Children Placed in Foster Homes.

43

Counselor Self-Awareness as the First Step in Counseling Preschool and Elementary Interracial Children and Their Families

Chapter 3 contained a section entitled The Counselor in a Working Relationship With an Interracial Individual or Family. As a first step in working with preschool and elementary interracial children and families, it is important for the counselor to review this section and engage in self-study and other awareness activities (Nishimura, 1995). As noted in Chapter 3, counselors who have not engaged in an examination of their feelings and attitudes toward all aspects of interracial relationships may inadvertently place too much emphasis on the interracial status of the child as an important aspect of problems faced by the interracial child, or they may completely ignore the possibility of considering the child's interracial status as any part of the problem.

Issues Faced by Many Interracial Children

One of the difficult tasks for the interracial child, adolescent, and adult is that of answering questions such as "Who are you?" or "What are you?" Interracial individuals experience both verbal and nonverbal communications requesting this information from an early age. The pressures to explain who and what one is continue throughout the individual's lifetime.

Interracial children may be objects of scrutiny by others or may be teased because of physical features (Adler, 1987; Lyles et al., 1985; McRoy & Freeman, 1986; Root, 1990; Steel, 1995; Wardle, 1993). Root (1990) explained how this extra attention can at first seem positive to young children. Invariably, however, children begin to feel negatively about this ongoing curiosity of others and may even begin to blame themselves for being different.

Interracial children may feel that they are outsiders and have to struggle for acceptance by both sides of their families. Williams (1995) recounts these painful experiences in his autobiography, *Life on the Color Line: The True Story of a White Boy Who Discovered He Was Black*. In an interview with David Aronson (1995), Michael Dorris described how being of mixed blood made him feel like an outsider trying to understand the behavior of both sides of his family and stated, "It's like being a foreigner in an odd kind of way, and it's very schizophrenic and painful for the child" (p. 11). Hutchinson (1990) relates a poignant story of an 11-year-old biracial Black/ American Indian boy who was rejected by both of his parents. The boy's statement that "Everybody has to be somewhere" (Hutchinson, 1990, p. 98) reflects the yearnings of many children with more than one racial heritage.

Comer (1988) underscores the importance of all children developing positive feelings about themselves and their own racial groups. He notes that "Negative or ambivalent feelings can cause difficult social, psychological, and eventually, economic consequences" (Comer, 1988, p. 167). When the child has more than one racial heritage, the challenges to developing positive feelings about all parts of one's racial heritage are compounded. Comer also cautions parents about the dangers to self and society when individuals develop chauvinistic attitudes about their own racial heritages.

In discussing therapy with a biracial child, Lyles et al. (1985) noted that raising a biracial child presented unusual challenges because of societal racism. Brandell (1988) seemed to support the viewpoint of Lyles et al. when he stated: "Biracial children, however, may have additional vulnerabilities because of the ambiguity of their racial status" (pp. 180–181).

The most significant issue faced by interracial children is the development of a positive racial identity. Interracial children may experience racial and ethnic identity development confusion because of a lack of age-appropriate information on their racial/ethnic heritages and because of the complexities of developing a positive interracial identity (Brandell, 1988; Root, 1990; Wardle, 1987, 1992a, 1993).

Adler (1987) states that "The development of a healthy identity is often at risk for the biracial child" (p. 57). He also notes that the stresses of parental adjustment to an interracial marriage or living arrangement may be severe. If the parents do not resolve these stresses and issues of their new identity, their children may be at special risk for behavioral and emotional problems. This possibility points to the need for the counselor to work with both the child and his or her family.

Because of societal pressures on some interracial children to identify only with their parent of color heritage, these children may be frustrated in developing a positive interracial identity (Funderburg, 1994; McRoy & Freeman, 1986; Steel, 1995; Wardle, 1992a, 1993). Bowles notes that "Failure to identify with one parent means that identification with that parent cannot be integrated as part of the biracial child's self-identity" (1993, p. 427). An additional issue discussed by Adler (1987) is the dilemma posed when interracial children perceive themselves to be one race and society views them as belonging to another race.

There may be a need for more and specialized adult nurturing to assist the interracial child in developing a positive self-concept (Adler, 1987; Brandell, 1988; McRoy & Freeman, 1986; Wardle, 1987, 1988a, 1988b, 1990, 1991, 1992a, 1993). It is often helpful to involve extended family members of both parents of the interracial child in activities to aid the child in developing positive feelings about her or his interracial heritage.

Contemporary Perspectives on the Racial/Cultural/Ethnic Identity Development of the Interracial Child

Historic perspectives on the racial and ethnic identity development of the interracial child were presented in Chapter 2. The following discussion first summarizes recent perspectives on the racial and ethnic identity development of the child from one racial heritage (Wehrly, 1995). A review of recent theories of identity development of interracial children follows.

The Child's Development of a Racial and Ethnic Identity

The cognitive developmental level of the child plays a large role in how the child understands and processes information (Thompson & Rudolph, 1992; Wehrly, 1995). Young children depend on concrete information and use absolutes and overgeneralizations to handle the large amount of race-related stimuli that have an impact on them

(Ramsey, 1987). They may suppress information that contradicts their overgeneralizations.

In the early stages of cognitive development, children face four blocks in their thought processes (Thompson & Rudolph, 1992). The *egocentrism block* causes children to believe that everyone views the world as they do and limits their ability to empathize with others. The *centration block* makes problem solving more difficult because they cannot focus on, or deal with, more than one part of the problem at once. Ramsey (1987) points out that this perspective is not the same as that of adults who intentionally say that people are all alike. The *reversibility block* makes children perception bound and unable to work from front to back and then back to front in problem solving. The *transformation block* limits children's abilities to see relationships between cause and effect and predict the consequences of their own behavior.

The child's cognitive development is not the only important aspect of how that child interprets environmental stimuli on racial matters. Children are very perceptive to affect in their environment; their racial attitudes, beliefs, and behaviors are influenced by both their cognitive development and the affective-laden statements of significant others (Phinney & Rotheram, 1987; Wehrly, 1995). The child who hears an important adult speak disparagingly of African Americans may generalize this negative attitude toward all individuals of that racial heritage and say something like "I don't like Black people." Katz (1987) believes that these aspects of the cognitive and affective development of children can result in prejudicial thinking about race.

The development of an ethnic identity by the child is a very complex process (Wehrly, 1995). Rotheram and Phinney (1987) describe the four components of this process as *ethnic awareness, ethnic self-identification, ethnic attitudes,* and *ethnic behaviors*. These four components are not mutually exclusive; they are interactive and overlapping.

Rotheram and Phinney (1987) define *ethnic awareness* as "the child's understanding of own and other ethnic groups" (p. 16). Ethnic awareness changes as the child has different experiences, is exposed to new information, and develops more advanced cognitive skills. As noted in the preceding section, the cognitive aspect of ethnic identity is influenced strongly by the affective and evaluative aspects of the child's life.

As children develop ethnic awareness they begin to notice obvious ethnic stimuli cues such as skin color, language, and customs. By the age of 3, both White and African American children can classify people as being Black or White, and these classification skills improve between the ages of 3 and 5 (Ramsey, 1987). Membership in a people of color group seems to make children more aware of ethnic stimuli than membership in the White population. Rotheram and Phinney (1987) observe that "many majority group children are not even aware that they belong to an ethnic group" (p. 17). Ethnic awareness precedes the ability to self-identify with an ethnic group.

Ethnic self-identification is a process that includes the ability to (a) recognize one's own group, (b) perceive that one is similar to others in that group, (c) be able to state the ethnic label for that group, and (d) apply this label consistently even with confusing stimuli cues (Rotheram & Phinney, 1987). Sometimes young children do not identify themselves correctly. We still do not know if children really *think* they belong to another group or *want* to belong to another group that they admire (Rotheram & Phinney, 1987). Ethnic self-identification is a complicated process because affect influences the social cognition component of this type of self-identification.

The two components of *ethnic attitudes* in children are their feelings about their own group and the feelings that they have about other groups (Rotheram & Phinney, 1987). The attitudes of people who are significant in the lives of children play a powerful role in the child's early socialization. Children are influenced by both verbal and nonverbal cues from the significant others in their environments as well as by attitudes in books read to them and in the media that they view (Katz, 1987).

As noted earlier, young interracial children are bombarded with questions about their heritage as well as inquisitive stares and other nonverbal signals from people in their environment (Root, 1990). Adler (1987) noted that biracial children "are often the object of scrutiny and curiosity [and] they experience the effects of racism at an early age" (p. 59).

It is from these socialization forces that children develop attitudes of liking or disliking themselves and people from their own and other ethnic groups. The seeds of prejudice and stereotypes are sown at a very early age through this cognitive and affective process (Katz, 1987; Ramsey, 1987; Rotheram & Phinney, 1987; Wehrly, 1995).

The development of *ethnic behaviors* is part of the child's socialization. The components of *ethnic awareness, ethnic self-identification*, and *ethnic attitudes* interact and result in ethnic behaviors. The values and behaviors of the group(s) in which children are socialized will play a powerful role in determining the ethnic behaviors of these children. An example of an ethnic behavior for a child of Native American heritage might be that the child will show respect for elders by looking down or away when speaking to older persons.

Learning ethnic behaviors is a complicated process for the child with one ethnic heritage. The process becomes increasingly complex for children with more than one ethnic heritage. For example, children whose biracial heritage is Native American and White may be confused as to whether they should look away or directly at the adults with whom they are speaking.

Challenges of Researching Racial and Ethnic Identity Development of the Interracial Child

The challenges of researching racial and ethnic identity in children have been increased by the overlap of issues of racial identity development, racial attitude development, and racial self-concept formation as well as interchangeable use of the terms *ethnic* and *race*. In addition, it is difficult to know how valid are the results of this research because of the lack of tight control on the use of age-appropriate questions and the many possible adult interpretations (or misinterpretations) of answers given by children.

McRoy and Freeman (1986) note the complexity of racial-identity development of mixed-race Black/White children because these children belong to one racial group that is valued positively by society and to one racial group that is viewed negatively by society. Johnson (1992a) believes that the biracial Black/White child has "dual minority status both within the larger society as a member of a partially devalued racial group and often within the African American community due to perceived lack of 'full' affiliation" (p. 45). Johnson (1992b) discusses the complexities of measuring racial preference and biculturality in biracial Black/White preschoolers.

Jacobs' Revised Model

As mentioned in the Historic section of Chapter 2, Jacobs has continued his research of the racial identity development of Black-White biracial children since his 1977 dissertation. Jacobs (1992) presents a detailed review and critique of more than 50 years of assessment of children's ethnic identity.

Jacobs also discusses the rationale for, and use of, a more suitable doll-play instrument to assess the child's ethnic identification. The doll interview developed by Jacobs includes these nine separate tasks: "1) story . . . . ; 2) matching . . . . ; 3) self-identification . . . . ; 4) family identification . . . . ; 5) preference, sibling . . . . ; 6) preference, play . . . . ; 7) preference, like/dislike . . . . ; 8) sibling of the light-brown boy doll . . . . ; and 9) constancy of racial identity" (1992, pp. 197–198). Jacobs stresses the importance of using terms and concepts originally introduced by the child during the interview.

In clinical use of the doll-play instrument, "Four factors emerged that were crucial in understanding the identity development of biracial children: (a) constancy of color, (b) internalization of an interracial or biracial label, (c) racial ambivalence, and (d) perceptual distortions in self- and family identifications" (Jacobs, 1992, p. 200). Based on research and clinical experience, Jacobs proposes that preadolescent biracial children progress through three stages in attaining biracial identity development. (Note that Jacobs added a stage since his earlier model [1977].) He recognizes that interracial identity development may differ for children whose interracial heritage is not Black-White. The three stages proposed by Jacobs are described as follows.

Stage I, Pre-Color Constancy: Play and Experimentation with Color (Jacobs, 1992). Biracial Black-White children under the age of about 4½ years are in the Pre-Color Constancy Stage. Most young interracial children engage in nonevaluative play with dolls of different colors in developing family constellations. They are able to identify their own color but do not show the ability to choose dolls of colors that are the same as the colors of other members of their families. Negative evaluations of color or refusal to engage in free play with dolls of different colors may occur in children with low self-esteem and with children who have been the victims of racial prejudice.

Stage II, Post-Color Constancy: Biracial Label and Racial Awareness (Jacobs, 1992). At about 4½ years of age, the young biracial Black-White child reaches the Post-Color Constancy Stage and realizes that his or her color will remain the same. It is during this stage that the Black-White biracial child begins to show ambivalence about his or her own racial status.

This sequential ambivalence usually shows first through preference for White and rejection of Black dolls followed by preference for Blackness and rejection of Whiteness. Sometimes biracial children displace this ambivalence onto Asian dimensions, either idealizing or scapegoating Asians.

Going through this stage of ambivalence is necessary for the biracial Black-White child so that "discordant elements can be reconciled in a unified identity" (Jacobs, 1992, p. 201). Children of different interracial heritages may experience similar stages of ambivalence toward the racial identities of their parents. Ambivalence toward their racial heritages gradually diminishes as interracial children move through the second stage of their identity development.

Children's racial self-concepts are based on the children's new understanding that their color will stay the same and their acquisition of a biracial or interracial label that they can internalize and "own." Biracial children seem to reach the color constancy stage on their own, but they may need help in acquiring a biracial or interracial label. Parents can help by talking with their children and giving them an interracial label that they can internalize and use

(Jacobs, 1977, 1992). In families where one or both of the parents are biracial, an appropriate multiracial or interracial label should be introduced.

Once children have adopted a biracial (or interracial) label, they construct their families in ways that acknowledge that their parents belong to different racial groups. At this stage interracial children will often show perceptual distortion in selecting colors to match their own color or that of siblings. Their choices in this color matching may be of colors darker than themselves or their siblings. Jacobs (1992) views these perceptual distortions as part of "the child's active attempts to understand racial class membership" (p. 20) and integral to the racial identity maturation process for the interracial child.

Stage III, Biracial Identity (Jacobs, 1992). Between the ages of 8 and 12 children discover that racial group membership is determined by the racial heritages of their parents. They also realize that (a) their skin color is correlated with their biracial or interracial heritages, (b) their race is not determined by their skin color, and (c) the different racial group memberships of their parents make them biracial or interracial. Parental efforts to help their children know both sides of their parentages equally are a great aid in the development of a biracial identity.

By Stage Three, children can separate skin color and racial group membership and make accurate choices of the skin color for themselves and other members of their families. The ambivalence toward the racial heritages of their parents that was present in the second stage continues to decrease and may be fully reconciled so that the child accepts a unified ego-identity. As the child enters adolescence, however, the old racial ambivalence may surface again as the young person restructures his or her sexual identity.

Jacobs (1992) stressed the importance of environmental and institutional influences on developing positive biracial identities when he stated, "The social, legal, and institutional acknowledgment of children's biracial group membership would facilitate the difficult task of constructing a positive biracial identity" (p. 206).

Biracial Identity Development Model Based on Kerwin's Qualitative Research

The purpose of Kerwin's doctoral dissertation (1991) was "to uncover the important variables for those who are directly involved with biracial identity development, Black/White interracially married parents, and their biracial offspring" (Kerwin, Ponterotto, Jackson, & Harris, 1993, p. 222). The difficulties of obtaining a larger sample for these audiotaped interviews are described by the authors of the 1993 manuscript reporting on Kerwin's qualitative study.

Interview guides were prepared by Kerwin (1991) in order to cover a broad range of topics in parent interviews as well as in the interviews with the children. At least one parent from each of the six Black-White families and nine children in these biracial households were interviewed.

The parent interview guide covered these topics: "family's identity, use/nonuse of an interracial label, racial awareness of child or children, dual socialization, family's coping skills, developmental issues and problems, sociocultural factors, and the role of schools" (Kerwin et al., 1993, p. 223). Themes from the interviews with parents will be discussed in Chapter 7, Counseling Interracial Families, and themes from interviews with adolescents will be reported in Chapter 5, Counseling Interracial Adolescents.

The children ranged in age from 5 to 16 years. Since six of these nine interviews were with children between 5 and 10 years of age, the report of research with this age grouping is summarized here. Categories covered in the interviews with the children were: "self-identity, use/nonuse of an interracial label, racial awareness, dual socialization, and the family's coping skills" (Kerwin et al., 1993, p. 223).

Themes from children in the 5- through 10-year-old category centered around labels, self-description, and racial awareness. Kerwin et al. (1993) did not perceive that the children in this study saw themselves as marginal. The young children were aware that people are of different colors and races and that it is possible to identify with more than one racial group.

Kerwin and Ponterotto (1995) present a six-stage model of biracial identity development based on findings reported in Kerwin (1991), Kerwin et al. (1993), and other empirical studies of biracial identity development. The first three stages of Kerwin and Ponterotto's model (1995) describe preschool and elementary children as follows:

Preschool. In the period up to 5 years of age, racial awareness develops for biracial children with an increasing perception of similarities and differences in people's appearance. Children growing up in a biracial family may develop racial awareness rather early if their parents expose them to different racial groups.

Entry to School. At this time biracial children begin to to be asked what they are. In response to these questions they define themselves and their families in descriptive terms. Some children define themselves by the color of their skin whereas others respond with a label such as *interracial*, especially if parents had taken the time to discuss self-identification labels with these children. Differences seem to occur at this stage depending on the representation of various racial groups in their school environment and the availability of Black and White models in the other milieus in which biracial children are socialized.

Preadolescence. In preadolescence biracial children become increasingly aware of the importance of skin color, physical appearance, and culture in determining group membership. Race, ethnicity, and religious background emerge as more important for self-labels than physical descriptors, however. At this developmental period, the biracial preadolescents are cognizant that their parents belong to different racial groups. Full awareness of their biracial status is often triggered by events such as entering a school that is racially integrated, moving to a school that is racially segregated, or experiencing racist behavior.

Clinical Case Study of an Interracial Child

Lyles et al. (1985) presented a contemporary case analysis of the identity development struggles of an 11-year-old child of Black and

White parentage raised in her biological White family. The child's obvious differences in physical appearance and the lack of support for her Black heritage led to the development of a very confused racial identity. She had not been given age-appropriate information about her parentage nor had she received positive emphasis on her dual racial heritage at an early age. The child suffered from teasing and ostracizing by family members and racial taunts at her predominantly White elementary school. She had great difficulties in developing friendships with other children. The case again illustrates the devastating results of the racism displayed by the significant others in the life of the child.

Counselor Roles in Work With Preschool and Elementary Interracial Children

As noted earlier, interracial children are subject to stares, statements, and questions from people who notice their different appearance. The way interracial children respond to this intrusion in their lives will be heavily influenced by how the family and other significant people in their lives have prepared these children for living with an interracial identity.

A case example of a biracial elementary school child, Joe, is presented first. Following this, counselor roles are discussed along with appropriate interventions to assist Joe.

CASE EXAMPLE

Joe is a 10-year-old biracial Black/White fourth grader whose family moved to the Thomas Jefferson Elementary School District during the summer. Early in the school year, Joe is referred to Mrs. Jones, the elementary school counselor at Thomas Jefferson School, because of fighting on the playground and lack of participation in classroom activities.

Thomas Jefferson School is located in an upper middle-class suburb of a large city. The student population is largely White with a small minority of Asian American and African American students. There are no other biracial fourth graders at the school. The administrative, teaching, and support personnel of the school are representative of the diversity of the nearby urban area.

Joe's mother is White and is a lawyer with a large downtown corporation. Joe's father is Black and is a surgeon at the nearby area hospital. Joe's parents work long hours at their respective jobs. An older brother is in high school and is an avid sports participant. Joe participates in an after-school program sponsored by the local YMCA. His older brother picks Joe up after football practice and is in charge of Joe until their parents arrive home from work.

In the first interview with Joe, Mrs. Jones learns that Joe feels lonesome for his old school and the friends he had there. Joe tells Mrs. Jones that on the playground, some of the other kids made fun of his kinky hair and tan skin. They asked him: "What are you, anyway?" Before Joe could answer, another boy called him the "N" word. This made Joe angry enough to fight the boy who called him the "N" word. Joe says he is embarrassed for fighting the boy and hopes Mrs. Jones will not tell his parents about the playground incident.

When Mrs. Jones asks Joe what is happening in his fourth grade classroom, Joe says the kids ignore him and he doesn't feel comfortable enough to volunteer in classroom discussions. The school records that were transferred from Joe's former school indicate that he was a very good student through Grade 3.

Counselor Roles in Work With School Personnel

The administrators, counselors, faculty, and other staff of preschool and elementary schools play a significant role in helping young interracial children develop positive feelings about their racial heritages (Wardle, 1990, 1992a, 1993). Counselors can play a leading role in helping to set a climate that celebrates the diversity and dignity of all children and their families.

It is important that the counselor establish a positive working relationship with all the people who work at the schools. One of the first steps in establishing this relationship requires the counselor to get out of his or her private office and to interact with children and all school personnel. Mrs. Jones makes it a point to be in the hall to interact with the elementary students and the school personnel before and after school. During the lunch period she sometimes has children bring their lunch to her office and meets with them over lunch. At other times, Mrs. Jones eats lunch with the teachers or in the cafeteria with students.

Counselors model a respect for individual differences and work with the rest of the school personnel to see that individual differences are validated, enjoyed, and celebrated. Mrs. Jones models respect for the diversity at Thomas Jefferson School through her daily interactions. She realizes that she can do more to see that individual differences are celebrated at Thomas Jefferson School, however, and arranges for pictures of all people who work at the school to be displayed on a bulletin board near the central office. Class pictures will be put on the wall beside the respective classroom doors (Wardle, 1992a, 1993).

Establishing a positive working relationship with teachers may involve (a) consulting with teachers about the needs of students, (b) working with teachers in in-service training, (c) assisting with in-classroom guidance activities, and (d) helping with parent conferences.

Mrs. Jones met with Joe's teacher when the teacher referred Joe for counseling. She will continue to meet with Joe's teacher, but she will be careful to reveal confidential information only with Joe's permission.

An important in-service topic for counselors to address is the process of helping all children develop positive feelings about their racial identities. Teachers at Thomas Jefferson realize that they know little about the process of racial identity development in children, especially the process for the interracial child. They have asked Mrs. Jones to offer an in-service workshop on racial identity development of children that will include information on the unique and complex path by which an interracial child develops a racial identity.

Mrs. Jones will present an in-service workshop that will include background information on children's development of racial identities and suggested activities to help all children develop pride in their racial heritage(s). A special section of the workshop will be tailored to understanding how interracial children move through the difficult period when they experience ambivalence toward their racial heritages and the stage marked by perceptual distortion of colors. The workshop will also address prejudice prevention activities.

Because Mrs. Jones presented a workshop in which teachers investigated their own racial and ethnic heritages the previous year, she believes they are ready for an in-service workshop on helping their students explore their racial backgrounds. At the close of last year's workshop, several of the teachers indicated that they were going to help their own children explore their family histories over the summer.

Teachers are locating materials on developing family trees. Two books that might be helpful to both teachers and students are *Do People Grow on Family Trees? Genealogy for Kids & Other Beginners* (Wolfman, 1991); and *Ethnic Pride: Explorations into Your Ethnic Heritage, Cultural Information, Activities, Student Research* (Lipson & Romatowski, 1983).

Parental cooperation will be enlisted through an article in the school newsletter that explains the class projects. The article will also address the role of racial/ethnic pride in the development of children's positive self-concepts. Parents will be encouraged to talk with Mrs. Jones or the school principal if they have concerns about having their children study their family's history.

One specific technique introduced in Chapter 3 that Mrs. Jones will suggest for classroom developmental multicultural guidance is bibliotherapy, the use of books for developmental or therapeutic purposes. The use of books to help interracial children have vicarious cross-cultural experiences may be particularly important for interracial children like Joe who live in ethnically isolated areas and who have limited opportunities to experience multicultural environments (Ponterotto, 1991). Books can also help other students at Thomas Jefferson broaden their world views on diversity.

The general considerations for use of bibliotherapy described in Chapter 3 can be applied in an age-appropriate or developmental level manner. A broad array of multicultural children's books (including some books with interracial characters) have been published in recent years. Appendix B of this book includes a listing of many interracial books, arranged by age level appropriateness.

Mrs. Jones will work with teachers in locating resources listing multicultural and interracial books for children (Camarata, 1991; Helbig & Perkins, 1994; Horning, 1993; Kruse, 1992; Roberts & Cecil, 1993). Annotations on many interracial books are noted in volumes of *The Bookfinder* (Dreyer, 1977, 1981, 1985, 1989, 1994) and in Capan (1994) and Capan and Suarez (1993).

Multicultural and interracial books are also included in Miller-Lachmann's *Our Family, Our Friends, Our World—An Annotated Guide to Significant Multicultural Books for Children and Teenagers* (1992). An introductory chapter addresses the need for a multicultural bibliography and the history of multicultural book publishing. Annotations on approximately 1,000 books published between 1970 and 1990 are included in the 18 chapters that follow. Each of the 18 chapters includes books representing a specific area of the world. The volume is unique in that it notes instances of biases and inaccuracies in the multicultural books. This information can be used to help readers "learn to read critically and to look behind stereotypes to the richness, diversity, and universal elements of each culture" (Miller-Lachmann, 1992, p. xi). A bright student like Joe may find it interesting to begin this process of reading critically.

Use of books for bibliotherapy will be most effective if the preschool or early elementary teacher and Mrs. Jones plan together to select the books, introduce the stories, and carry out follow-up activities. Some counselors have tape-recorded the stories so that they can show the book's pictures and watch the nonverbal reactions of the child or children listening to the story and viewing the pictures. The tape can be turned off for discussion at appropriate times. Hearing the stories and seeing the pictures can help young interracial children realize that other boys and girls live in families like theirs where the mother and father are of different racial heritages.

The story content and the reader can also help the listeners realize that the characters in the story may be facing mixed feelings about their interracial heritage. Children are encouraged to verbalize feelings about their unique family situations. The counselor can help to validate these feelings as "OK" and assist children in learning the difference between having feelings and acting negatively on feelings.

Preschoolers and early elementary children can also be introduced to various labels that families in the stories give to their interracial situations. Discussion of the various labels used by mixed-race families can follow. This may help children with more than one racial heritage move through Jacobs's second stage of interracial identity development, Post-Color Constancy, Biracial Label, and Racial Ambivalence.

Other activities such as writing a different ending to the story can be added to the use of bibliotherapy with cognitively more mature children, like Joe, who can read the stories on their own. Careful choice of appropriate stories to meet the needs of the children and timing of the reading of the stories are still important first steps. The choice of follow-up activities is especially important in increasing the effectiveness of bibliotherapy. Some follow-up activities might include: (a) use of open-ended questions related to the content of the story and about the feelings of the characters in the story, (b) discussions about times when the listeners or readers related to the feelings of the children in the story, (c) completion of unfinished sentences, (d) role playing of segments of the story with discussions of feelings experienced while role playing, (e) participation in art activities, and (f) formulation and discussion of different endings to the story (Cornett & Cornett, 1980).

Rosenberg's 1986 photoessay, *Living in Two Worlds*, will be presented for possible use for classroom bibliotherapy in all of the fourth grades at Thomas Jefferson School. In this story, people in four interracial families tell the advantages and challenges of growing up in mixed heritage families. Children are introduced to the way these families celebrate differences in languages, religions, food, clothing, and cultural traditions. The interracial children in *Living in Two Worlds* speak of how they feel when insensitive questions and remarks are made to them. On his own, Joe is reading *All But the Right Folks* (Nichols, 1985) and will discuss it with Mrs. Jones at the next session.

For teachers interested in developing multicultural classroom guidance units, a chapter by Omizo and D'Andrea (1995) will be suggested. This chapter provides a rationale for multicultural classroom guidance and outlines a 16-session multicultural guidance program that has been tested on fifth graders. The authors note that the classroom guidance program can be modified for use as early as third grade or for use with older children.

Two other examples of the many books available for classroom diversity projects are *Americans, Too! Understanding American Minorities through Research-Related Activities* (Aten, 1982), and *Multi-Cultural Art Projects* (Griswold & Starke, 1987). *Teaching Tolerance*, a free magazine that contains a wealth of stories and ideas for promoting multiculturalism and diversity in the schools, will be available to teachers. It is published twice yearly by the Southern Poverty Law Center, 400 Washington Avenue, Montgomery, Alabama 36104.

Frances Wardle, one of the proponents of classroom interventions for biracial children, underscores the importance of teacher sensitivity to the identity development needs of interracial children. The teachers at Thomas Jefferson School will find Wardle's suggestions enlightening and invaluable in working with interracial children and their families (Wardle, 1987, 1988a, 1988b, 1990, 1991, 1992a, 1993; Wardle & Baptiste, 1988).

Mrs. Jones will continue to work with teachers in locating materials for other classroom diversity activities (Henderson, 1990). She has offered to co-lead classroom sessions on diversity.

Teachers and staff will work with Mrs. Jones to identify interracial individuals in the community and to enlist their cooperation as resource people for career development forums and projects (J. Johnson, personal communication, March 19, 1995). There can be great value in having the interracial students see and talk with interracial adults who serve as models for them.

Mrs. Jones is also prepared to facilitate in-service training on culturally sensitive active listening. Faculty and staff who have already experienced this training will be invited to serve as co-facilitators for the in-service workshop. Learning and practicing the skills of culturally sensitive active listening can greatly magnify positive working relationships throughout the school and can help children feel personal attention from the adults at their school.

On the bulletin board outside of her office, Mrs. Jones will display a collage that shows every kind of family: "foster, adoptive, two-parent, single-female headed family, single male-headed family, interracial, extended, and minority" (Wardle, 1992a, p. 169). Families representing these different varieties of current familial composition will be invited to the classrooms. Nishimura (1995) notes that "It is equally important for monoracial children to be exposed to diverse family configurations so that they begin to see differences as being normal" (p. 55). Multicultural and diversity projects will be ongoing throughout the school year so that the celebration of a particular ethnic group is not limited to one day, week, or month. The developmental multicultural program has been put together by a teacher committee and Mrs. Jones and approved by the administration and school board.

Mrs. Jones has already visited all of the classrooms to explain her role to the children in age-appropriate language. Limits on confidentiality have been clarified. Time was allowed for the children to ask questions and for Mrs. Jones to explain the process by which they may self-refer.

As a member of the School Advisory Committee, Mrs. Jones is working with the committee to revise registration forms that request the racial identity of children. School personnel are aware of the need for this revision since other interracial families are moving into the school district. Adding the category of "mixed race" or "interracial" will help interracial children realize that all parts of their racial heritage are important.

Counseling With Interracial Children

Adler (1987) states: "The most important goal in counseling biracial students is to increase awareness of their heritage and to enhance the dignity and respect given to that heritage" (p. 58). Building the cross-cultural relationship with the interracial child may be challenging for the counselor, especially if this is the first time the child has seen a counselor or if the child is not a self-referral. Because there was an elementary counselor at Joe's former school and Mrs. Jones has already visited his classroom, establishing a relationship with Joe was not a challenge.

Mrs. Jones will draw on her training in cross-cultural counseling to work with Joe, an interracial child. She is aware of the misuse of cultural knowledge with any client and that we "walk a tightrope" in use of cultural information in cross-cultural counseling (Wehrly, 1991, 1995). If we have no information on the cultures of our clients, we may make blunders in counseling that can destroy the cross-cultural working relationship. If we use the cultural information that we have to stereotype our clients, we deny their uniqueness as individuals and may insult or demean them (Kleinman, 1985). These cautions apply, also, to cross-cultural work with children. An insensitive assumption that might be made in work with an interracial Black/White child such as Joe would be to tell him that you expect that the family enjoys eating "chitlins and collards" rather than asking Joe about his food preferences.

It is assumed that the counselor will consider the cognitive developmental level of the child in selection of counseling techniques and interventions. If the child has any physical limitations, the counselor may also need to consider these in working with that child. Joe is a bright fourth grader and has no physical limitations, so Mrs. Jones will be able to use a variety of counseling techniques with him.

Because Joe was referred to the counselor by his teacher, an age-appropriate discussion of the referral was included in the first session. Mrs. Jones explained the teacher's referral in positive terms, stating that Joe's teacher thought he might profit from talking with a counselor. Then she asked Joe to tell her how he felt about being referred to a counselor. Joe stated that he felt somewhat nervous but knew that the counselor was there to help.

There are special issues to consider in working with interracial children, but the counselor must remember that the problem with which the interracial child needs help may be unrelated to her or his interracial status (Wardle & Baptiste, 1988). As noted in Chapter 3, racial identity problems were *not* listed among presenting problems for the majority of mixed-race children referred to school social workers (McRoy & Freeman, 1986; Nishimura, 1995). Instead, mixed-race children were more often referred for problems of academic achievement, inattentiveness in the classroom, social isolation, negative attitudes toward adults, or aggressive behavior toward peers. School counselors can expect similar reasons for referrals of mixed-race children to them.

Joe's referral to the counselor *is* related to his interracial status and the aggressive behavior Joe displayed when he felt insulted by a peer. Joe's teacher also expressed concern over Joe's withdrawn behavior in the classroom.

Joe has already expressed regret for fighting in response to feeling insulted. Mrs. Jones may encourage more exploration of Joe's feelings about this incident if Joe wishes to discuss it. It will be important to determine how Joe has responded in the past when he has been asked the question, "What are you, anyway?" This discussion can lead into an exploration of Joe's personal feelings about his racial identity and whether he has talked with his parents about this. Alternative responses to questions on racial identity can be explored and role played during counseling sessions.

One of the most valuable tools that any counselor with children has is the ability to listen actively. In the busy world in which today's children live, it may be rare for them to have an adult listen actively to them for even a few minutes. Through culturally sensitive active listening, the counselor can gain a perspective on how interracial children view their worlds and how they feel about the situations in which they live. Because Joe is new to the community and still misses his old friends, he is especially appreciative of the opportunity to talk freely with an understanding person like Mrs. Jones.

The use of feeling reflections and open-ended questions are often conducive to helping children talk more freely about their problems. Strong feelings about children's interracial identity need to be heard and validated. Brandell (1988) states that some interracial children who have rejected the racial heritage of one of their parents may display massive feelings of guilt as well as feelings of disloyalty. The feelings of ambivalence described by Jacobs (1977, 1992) are common. Joe has already moved through the stage where he felt ambivalent about his dual racial heritage and sequentially showed preference for his White mother and then for his Black father. He no longer shows perceptual distortion in identifying the skin coloring of other members of his family. Joe does remember feeling guilty about rejecting his White mother during the stage when he identified only with his Black father. He and Mrs. Jones have discussed whether this guilt still bothers him.

Interracial children like Joe may be the targets of racist behaviors. At times the counselor's role will be to help children sort out the reality of racist behaviors in other people. The counselor and Joe have discussed when and how to stand up to people who direct racist behaviors toward him. Joe let Mrs. Jones know that when his peers call him racist names in the future, he will let them know he thinks they are trying to hurt him. He is also willing to tell his peers and adults that he is mixed Black and White because his father is Black and his mother is White. Role playing and role reversal were valuable in teaching Joe when and how to use these responses. Concurrent classroom discussions on racism and antiracist behavior are occurring to help all children understand their roles in reducing racism in the school environment.

The counselor may need to sort out the reticence of some children to talk about problems to determine if there is a cultural component that has conditioned these children to show respect through silence or not sharing family secrets with anyone outside of the family. A cultural impact on nonverbal communication and on the use of space may also be evident. Joe does not seem reluctant to talk about his problems, so Mrs. Jones does not see a need to explore cultural influences on talking about personal problems.

Joe tells Mrs. Jones that his family rarely talks about race or racial issues. He thinks it is because his mother and father are so busy with their demanding occupations. Joe says that his grandparents are "neat people" and show lots of love for him. He rarely gets to see his grandparents, however, because they live hundreds of miles away. Joe knows that Mrs. Jones will be meeting with his parents. He has given her permission to tell them he would like to have more family discussions on race and how to handle racist behaviors.

In individual counseling with interracial children, Mrs. Jones finds play media helpful with those who are reticent to talk. Some girls and boys enjoy working with clay; others express themselves well through art activities. Crayons and paints in shades of different skin, hair, and eye colors should be available if the counselor is going to have children use art media. If the counselor uses family figures, it will be very important for the child to have access to family figures in various skin color shades and with features representing all people of color groups. Joe loves to draw pictures and is enjoying drawing while he talks with Mrs. Jones.

School counselors rarely have time to engage in in-depth or extended therapy with children. When children manifest problems that need more time or expertise than the counselor can give, they are referred to a mental health center where counselors have appropriate background for evaluation and follow-up treatment of interracial children.

Many of the problems manifested by interracial children brought for therapy are related to the racial identity confusion felt by the interracial child even though the verbalized presenting problem(s) may not indicate this (Brandell, 1988). This seems to be particularly true with interracial children whose parents are divorced or separated and who rarely, or never, see the absent parent or any of the absent parent's extended family. Often the interracial child has been raised almost solely with people of the racial heritage of the parent with whom the child lives. In cases like this, it is especially important for the counselor to take time to listen to the child and the adult who has brought the child for therapy. Assessing how interracial children view their racial identity will be important. Working with both the child and significant adults in the child's life may be necessary in the assessment.

Brandell (1988) describes psychoanalytic self-psychology therapy with a biracial Black-White child referred mainly because of escalating behavior problems at school and hostile and defiant behaviors at home. According to Brandell (1988), the child was suffering from ongoing empathic failures of her parents, especially "traumatic disappointments in her father" (p. 185). The child's father had left a live-in relationship with her mother before the child was born. He was erratic in keeping promises to spend time with the child. Brandell gives a detailed account of the techniques and processes that he used in therapy with this interracial child. The most effective techniques were reciprocal drawing and storytelling games. The use of the self-psychological perspective helped the therapist identify problems in self-identity development of the interracial child.

Counselor Work With Parents and Families of Interracial Children

As Wardle (1990) notes, parents in interracial families are raising their children in a variety of ways: as "just children" with no attention given to their racial identity, as children with one racial identity (sometimes that of the people of color parent), or as children with a rich interracial status. Children of interracial heritage have genes from both parents and from the racial heritages of both parents. The genes from one parent do not dominate the genes from the other parent.

Identity development, including racial identity development, begins in early childhood and continues throughout the individual's life. The child's physical appearance will have an important role in the child's racial identity development. For many interracial children, skin color differences may be one of the first differences they notice about themselves and others. Parents play an important role in how well the interracial child is able to accept her or his physical appearance.

Counselors and teachers working with interracial children should meet with parents to discuss some issues that are unique to the interracial family. Mrs. Jones has asked Joe's parents to meet with her. Because both of them are busy during the day, Mrs. Jones will meet with them during the evening sessions scheduled for parent conferences for teachers. After talking with them about their perspectives on Joe, Mrs. Jones plans to use some of Wardle's (1990) questions in her conference with Joe's parents:

1. How do the people in your home identify your interracial children?
2. How is Joe's interracial status supported and nurtured in the home?

3. What do you, as Joe's parents, want the school staff to do to support your choice for Joe's interracial identity?
4. How do you respond to negative comments directed at your sons by other children or by adults? How are you teaching Joe to respond to these negative comments?
5. What do those in the home do to "positively reaffirm your children's differences [to Joe]?" (Wardle, 1990, p. 25).

Parents can be encouraged to offer age-appropriate answers to questions their interracial children ask. Emphasis on positive aspects of the child's interracial heritage is important (Lyles et al., 1985). This information should be given in a straightforward manner as soon as children become racially aware and raise concerns about their racial heritages.

Counselors can help validate and support a family lifestyle that celebrates the interracial family heritage (Adler, 1987). Parents can be encouraged to help their children reach an awareness of the racial and ethnic cultures of both mother and father. Because Joe's grandparents live some distance away, his parents can be encouraged to participate with Joe in cultural activities to acquaint him with both sides of his racial heritage.

Joe has asked Mrs. Jones to let his parents know that he would like them to take time to talk about race in family discussions. She will do this and encourage them to discuss ways they might implement these discussions. Mrs. Jones is prepared to respond to questions that Joe's parents may have on this issue. She will show empathy for their long working hours and the resulting difficulty in finding time for family discussions, but she will also stress the importance of these opportunities for family communication.

As noted earlier in this chapter, Jacobs (1977, 1992) describes two kinds of information that parents can present to their children to help the children's biracial identity development. First, parents can help their children to see that they are part of both parents and part of the race of each of these parents. Children can be taught that they are part _____ and part _____ . In addition, biracial parents can teach their children that they (the children) are different from the race of either parent. Parents can help their children decide on a biracial or interracial identity such as "I'm mixed," "I'm biracial," "I'm interracial," or "I'm multiracial." Use of the questions suggested by Wardle should help Mrs. Jones determine what Joe's parents have done, or are doing, to address these issues with their son.

Parents may need assistance in understanding and working with the racial ambivalence that biracial children normally show between the ages of about 4½ and 8 years of age. It may help parents to know that "The working through of ambivalence seems primarily influenced by parents' supportive interest in the child's racial feelings and secondarily by a racially supportive environment outside of the family" (Jacobs, 1992, p. 205). This underscores the importance of a biracial or multiracial environment for the interracial child. Mrs. Jones may want to find out how Joe's parents helped their sons through this difficult stage.

Counselors sometimes educate the interracial family through making them aware of support groups, recommending appropriate books to use with their interracial children (see Appendix B), and helping families develop approaches for addressing myths related to interracial individuals and families. Joe's parents share with Mrs. Jones that they participated in an active interracial support group in the area in which they previously lived. They intend to continue with this group even though it is now a greater distance to drive to meetings. Mrs. Jones may explore the possibility of Joe's parents helping to get a new interracial support group started in the community where they now live.

Special Considerations for Counseling Interracial Children in Foster Homes

The literature on the placement of interracial children in foster or adoptive homes is almost nonexistent. Some families become interracial through trans- or cross-racial adoption. Chapter 7 will include a section on work with families that have become interracial through adoption. Joe and his family did not "fit" in this category, but counselor awareness of these considerations will be important to Mrs. Jones and the faculty at her school.

Folaron and Hess (1993) report on a longitudinal study of foster home placements of 10 mixed African American and Caucasian children through the child welfare system. Their findings raise serious questions about the child welfare system's ability to identify and address the needs of children of mixed African American and Caucasian heritage. The authors express concerns related to assessing the feelings and special needs of parents of interracial children. Questions were also raised about the adequacy of selecting and preparing potential foster homes for the interracial children.

The need to confront and challenge "the social, institutional, and personal racism that undermines quality placement experiences and services to families" (Folaron & Hess, 1993, p. 124) is discussed. A systemic approach that includes consideration of the child, the child's family, the potential foster family, and the community environment of the potential foster family is recommended.

In addition to issues and concerns already discussed, mixed-race children in foster homes may have a strong feeling of insecurity that manifests itself through compensatory negative behaviors. Foster home interracial children may feel lonely and rejected, especially if they have moved repeatedly within the foster home system with conditions precluding a return to their parental home.

School counselors can be involved in several roles to assist foster home children of mixed heritage. Counselors can provide a real service to these young people by working with them on an individual or small-group basis. Small-group work can have the advantage of helping the foster home interracial child build friendships. By working with teachers and foster parents, school counselors can help interracial children experience a more secure and predictable environment.

Summary

This chapter discussed several counseling roles with preschool and elementary interracial children. The need for counselors to engage in self-examination of their own beliefs, attitudes, and behaviors toward interracial friendships, unions, and children was reiterated. The challenges of developing positive racial identities and positive self-concepts were identified as significant issues faced by many interracial children.

Current theories of children's cognitive, affective, and interracial identity development provided the basis for a discussion of counselor roles with Joe (a hypothetical interracial fourth grader), the school personnel, and Joe's parents. The chapter closed with a discussion of special considerations for counseling interracial children placed in foster homes.

5

Counseling Interracial Adolescents

The magnitude of the task for counselors who are working with interracial adolescents is summarized by Gibbs (1987) as that of helping the adolescent "to integrate the dual racial identifications into a single identity that affirms the positive aspects of each heritage, acknowledges the reality of societal ambivalence, and rejects the self-limitations of racial stereotypes of behavior on the process of self-actualization" (pp. 275–276). This chapter presents background information on interracial adolescents and discusses the many roles in which counselors may be involved in helping interracial adolescents achieve positive self-identities.

Topics related to the counselor's roles with interracial adolescents are discussed under these subheadings: Counselor Self-Awareness as the First Step in Counseling Interracial Adolescents, Issues Faced by Interracial Adolescents, Contemporary Perspectives on the Racial/Cultural/Ethnic Identity Development of Interracial Adolescents, Counselor Roles in Work With Interracial Adolescents, and Special Considerations for Counseling Interracial Adolescents in Foster or Adoptive Homes.

Counselor Self-Awareness as the First Step in Counseling Interracial Adolescents

Counselors who work with interracial adolescents, their families, or both need to engage in in-depth self-examination of their own racial/ethnic identity development. Of particular importance is self-examination of one's values and attitudes toward interracial dating, interracial couples, interracial unions, and the offspring of interracial unions. Nishimura (1995) states that school counselors must ask themselves what assumptions they have regarding interracial marriages and biracial children and consider how these assumptions may influence "diversity celebration themes promoted in developmental counseling programs" (p. 55).

A process for counselor self-examination is delineated in Chapter 3 under the section Counselor Self-Study of Ethnic/Racial Heritage. A review of this process is recommended for those who have given little thought to the impact of their own values and biases on their work with the interracial population.

Issues Faced by Interracial Adolescents

Adolescence is an especially vulnerable time for many interracial individuals because identity issues become racial problems when the interracial person starts dating (Poussaint, 1984; Root, 1994). All dating is potentially interracial for these adolescents (Root, 1990, 1994). An interracial Caucasian-Jamaican young woman interviewed by Funderburg (1994) supported this when she told how she had no problems with friendships before adolescence. She was attending a private school that was all White, so all her friends were White. When this young adolescent started going to parties, she began to feel uncomfortable. "As soon as dating and going to dances came up, that's when I started having problems" (Funderburg, 1994, p. 37).

Gibbs (1987) and Overmier (1990) state that the important questions for these biracial teenagers seem to be "Who am I?" and "Where do I fit?" In adolescence the question of social acceptance is paramount. Biracial female adolescents report anxiety over social acceptance based on exclusion from groups in which they were accepted as children. There is an abrupt recognition of the need to redefine and renegotiate their social relationships and status. The process of finding friends who will accept them as unique individuals and show them unconditional acceptance can be a painful one for some biracial adolescents of either sex.

The need for interracial adolescents to redefine relationships is related to societal racism (both overt and covert) and its impact on the youth of more than one racial heritage. "For some biracial persons this will be the first time that they experience barriers because of color or their socially perceived ambiguous race" (Root, 1990, p. 195). In the process of redefining relationships, many interracial adolescents are called upon to deal with stereotypes, prejudice, and racism on a regular basis.

Another major issue that is frequently reported by interracial adolescents is the problem of choosing what racial or ethnic identity label fits for them (Gibbs & Hines, 1992). Peer and societal pressures to choose one identity may be great. Parents may or may not help supply an interracial label.

Steel (1995) recalls how difficult it was to claim both the White identity of her father and the Ghanaian African identity of her mother. By her sophomore year in high school in the Washington, D.C., area, Steel realized that no matter how she tried to identify herself, she was seen as Black. During the summer between her sophomore and junior years in high school she returned to Ghana with her mother to visit family. As they walked the streets of the capital city and small villages of Ghana, people stared at her openly and kept saying "Oburoni" (White person). This made Steel realize that although she had as much White as African heritage, her identity depended on which side of the Atlantic Ocean she was on and what part of her identity people saw. Steel (1995) stated "there was nothing arbitrary about my personal identity. . . . I knew who I was. . . . What was arbitrary was other people's constructions of race and how they perceived me" (p. 49). She was able to reconcile this dilemma through developing pride in being different from what was expected of her.

Gibbs (1989) underscores the powerful influence of societal forces on biracial Black-White youth in her statement: "Biracial children and adolescents are particularly vulnerable to differential treatment by their parents and relatives, social rejection by their peers, and ambivalent attention in their schools and communities" (p. 327). Hatcher (1987) reported on interviews with seven interracial young people and noted that schools "dealt with these youngsters as single race individuals, typically the race of the minority parent" (p. 203).

Root (1990) describes how "tokenism," a form of racism, may surface during adolescence for the interracial young person. Members of the dominant group may feel less threatened by the values and appearance of the interracial young person and hire this individual to satisfy a person of color quota. Root states that the people doing the hiring err in two ways. First, they use the interracial individual to avoid their own racism; second, they do not give the interracial person the choice of stating his or her racial identity.

Other problems related to development of a positive biracial identity are those of ambiguities over gender identity or sexual orientation, issues related to the development of autonomy, and conflicts related to educational and occupational aspirations (issues faced by many monoracial adolescents). These issues are discussed in the section of this chapter entitled Research of Gibbs and Associates. The challenges of separating issues related to biracial identity development from normal developmental task issues for adolescents can be difficult.

Contemporary Perspectives on the Racial/Cultural/Ethnic Identity Development of Interracial Adolescents

In Chapter 2, Erik Erikson (1950, 1963, 1968) was credited with laying the groundwork for psychological perspectives on adolescent identity development. Erikson helped us to understand that adolescence is a critical period for the establishment of a clear and stable sense of identity. Although he did not directly address racial or ethnic identity problems of interracial youth, Erikson did call attention to the enormous challenges that would be faced by the non-White adolescent who was the victim of racism from the dominant White majority group. Developing this stable, single identity with a dual- or multiracial heritage that reflects positive aspects of both (or all) heritages and rejects societal self-limiting stereotypes can be an even larger task.

Hoare (1991) expands on the concepts of Erikson and other social psychologists and presents issues that are thought provoking as they relate to the racial/cultural/ethnic identity development of interracial adolescents. She notes that "adolescents seem to begin identity formation establishing who they are and eliminating who they are not before they can move forward developmentally" (Hoare, 1991, p. 47). In addition, Hoare (1991) posits that "The Western norm of individualism, when grounded in adolescent autonomy and in repudiation of persons and groups different from the in-group, tends to abet prejudice" (p. 49). Consider the conflicting feelings and heart-rending choices that this repudiation may generate in the adolescent with more than one racial heritage.

The next sections summarize research on racial/cultural/ethnic identity development of interracial adolescents. Some of the research has been with college-age interracial youth and includes not only adolescents but young adults as well.

Research of Gibbs and Associates

In 1986 Gibbs surveyed 50 San Francisco Bay Area social service, mental health, special education, and probation agencies (Gibbs, 1987) and found that 60% of the 31 agencies responding stated that referrals of biracial adolescents had increased in the 10 years previous to the study and that biracial adolescents were overrepresented in the populations they served. Gibbs also reviewed three other sources of clinical information that indicated that these youth have unique problems and needs. Poussaint (1984) was recognized as describing positive adjustments and successful goal attainment by biracial youth.

From her decade-long studies of clinical observations of biracial youth, Gibbs (1987, 1989) developed a model listing these five potential areas for biracial adolescent identity development conflicts: (a) conflicts associated with dual racial heritage, (b) conflicts related to feeling socially marginal, (c) conflicts about impulse and sexual management, (d) conflicts related to autonomy issues with parents, and (e) conflicts over educational and career aspirations (Gibbs, 1987, 1989). Gibbs recognized that monoracial youth experience some of the same conflicts but noted that the symptoms and behavior may come from different sources.

Fairly consistent patterns of defense mechanisms and coping strategies were observed in the biracial youth in psychological treatment. Defense mechanisms varied between polar reactions and appeared in these forms: rejecting or denying of either their Black or their White heritage, overidealizing of either their White or Black heritage, consistently identifying with the aggressor in interpersonal situations, sublimating or repressing sexual or aggressive feelings, premature separating from parents or lacking individuation from parents, and overcompensating or consistently engaging in self-derogation in school or work settings.

Following the study of youth in clinical settings, Gibbs and her associates began a 2-year study of the psychosocial adjustment of a sample of *nonclinical* Black-White adolescents and their parents (Gibbs & Hines, 1992). The study of 10 families with 12 adolescents focused on: (a) the process that these biracial young people experience in forming a stable ethnic identity, and (b) their parents' perceptions of how these adolescents are coping in an interracial family. The 12 Black-White young people in this study participated in these assessments: the Biracial Adolescent Psychosocial Interview, the Achenbach Youth Self-Report, and the Rosenberg Self-Esteem Scale for Adolescents. Parents were requested to fill out a Parents' Questionnaire.

A large amount of rich data were gathered in the responses from the 12 nonclinical biracial teens and their parents. Highlights are reported under Gibbs's model of five potential areas for adolescent identity development conflict.

The following *conflicts related to their racial/ethnic identity* were reported by the 12 nonclinical biracial teens. Identifying completely with the racial and cultural background of the White parent led to rejection of the racial and cultural background of the Black parent. Overidentifying with the Black parent led to the adoption of "stereotyped minority behaviors and a negative identity" (Gibbs & Hines, 1992, p. 229). Others showed ambivalent feelings about the racial and cultural background of both parents and would alternately accept and reject the values, beliefs, and behaviors of both groups. Some teens felt pressured to identify with one group or the other. Others noted that they held "divided loyalties" and that situational and environmental demands brought out behaviors related to the culture in which they were functioning.

The question, "How do you think about yourself racially?" brought varying results. Six (50%) identified as mixed race; two (16.7%) identified as Black; one (8.3%) identified as African American; and two (16.7%) did not know how they would answer this question. (Parent reports indicated that 60% of the parents said they taught their children that they were Black and labeled their children as Black when filling out forms.) When the young people were asked "how they generally labelled themselves, the majority of eight (66.7%) replied 'mixed'" (Gibbs & Hines, 1992, p. 230).

In response to what they liked about being biracial, teens reported appearance, being unique and different, and being able to fit in with all teen groups. Things the teens did not like about being biracial were name calling, their minority status, and being conspicuous. Difficulties in growing up as biracial children were reported by more than half of the adolescents. Slightly more than half had grown up with exposure to both races. The same number (7) mentioned that there had been some discussion on racial and ethnic differences in their homes but that they would like more frequent discussion of racial and ethnic identity issues with their families.

The questions related to *social marginality* brought thoughtful information. All of the teens attended racially mixed high schools and all had some non-White teachers, but none reported having teachers who identified themselves as mixed or biracial. All of these biracial teens felt positive about relationships with their peers at school, and two thirds reported getting along very well with class-mates. Slightly less than half (5) said they enjoyed school. When asked about what they did not like at school, only two of the teens stated that they were treated unfairly by their teachers. Three fourths of the biracial teens participated in school activities, and three fourths of them worked part-time outside of school.

Gibbs and Hines (1992) summarized by stating "the majority of this group appeared to be comfortable with their social identity as biracial persons and had established positive relations with Black, White, and other mixed-race and minority peers" (p. 232).

Under the category *conflicts about sexuality*, all 12 of the teens indicated that they would date Black, biracial, or Hispanic individuals. Nearly half of the individuals had no preference for the race of the person they would date. They indicated a range of behaviors related to their sexuality. The rate of teen sexual activity (about one-third) was consistent with recent estimates for this age group. The authors noted that these teens did not have difficulties managing their impulses, but some of the subjects seemed to be socially immature. Female biracial teens were somewhat more likely than males to have concerns about dating and being sexually active.

Conflicts over autonomy and independence are normal for all teenagers and may be increasingly problematic for teens growing up in an interracial family. Tensions related to these aspects of being a biracial teenager seemed to be normative with teenagers in a monoracial family. Nearly all of them believed they got along well with their mothers and about half of them reported good relations with their fathers. It should be noted that half of these biracial teens did not live with their fathers. Overall, the biracial *nonclinical* teens seemed to show the same concerns about parental expression of affection or overprotection as other young biracial teens.

In the realm of *conflicts over educational and career aspirations*, no major problems surfaced. Three fourths of these biracial teens were performing above average academically and were planning to go to college and graduate school. It appeared that their biracial identity had not affected their future aspirations negatively, nor had it foreclosed options for them.

In summarizing *general psychosocial adjustment*, Gibbs and Hines noted that self-esteem scores for these biracial teens were above average as compared with all teenagers. They used alcohol and drugs infrequently. Scores on the Youth Self-Report Inventory were within the normal range for non–clinic-referred teenagers.

In an overall summary, Gibbs and Hines (1992) noted that this study of the biracial teens not in counseling produced a somewhat different picture than the results of previous studies of biracial teens in psychological treatment. Three fourths of the nonclinical biracial teens felt comfortable with their biracial identity, had learned to negotiate and cherish positive aspects of both their Black and White heritages, got along well with their peers, did well in managing sexual and aggressive impulses, achieved a healthy separation from their parents, and had established appropriate educational and career goals.

Twenty-five percent of the nonclinical biracial teenage group did show problematic psychosocial adjustment. In comparison with the 75% that displayed good adjustment, this group had lower self-esteem scores, more ambivalence about being labeled Black, increased levels of sexual and social immaturity, and confusion about career and life goals.

Biracial Identity Development Model for Adolescents and Young Adults Based on Kerwin's Research

Three of the children studied by Kerwin (1991) were teenagers. All reported that they had been asked about their racial identity. These young people had learned to handle the situation well by answering that they were "mixed," and, if queried more, the teenagers responded that one parent was Black and one parent was White.

These biracial teens could all recall times when they had been pressured (usually by peers) to choose the values and behaviors of one color over the other. They did not report feeling marginal, but one did say that she feels "in the middle" when conflicts arise between Black and White groups at her school. It appeared that this pressure to go with a people of color group occurred more for the females than the males. The 16-year-old male in this group attributed the greater compatibility of the males in his school to the fact that they all play together in sports.

Adolescence is the fourth stage of the Kerwin-Ponterotto model of biracial identity development (Kerwin & Ponterotto, 1995). These authors recognize that adolescence is often the most difficult time for the biracial youth because racial identity development becomes such an important part of overall identity development. In-groups and out-groups become increasingly evident with many biracial adolescents feeling pressured into choosing one racial identification over the other. Other reference group orientations, such as special academic interests or participation in sports, may neutralize the pressures to choose one racial group over the other.

College/young adulthood is the fifth stage of the Kerwin-Ponterotto model of biracial identity development. Young biracial adults may continue to immerse themselves in one culture while totally rejecting the culture of their other racial heritage. As the young biracial adult matures, however, there is a greater tendency to reject the expectations of others to choose one culture over the other. The individual grows in awareness and acceptance of the fact that she or he is biracial and bicultural.

If the biracial individual has been successful in working through the five stages, "there will be a growing recognition of the advantages as well as the disadvantages associated with having a biracial heritage" (Kerwin & Ponterotto, 1995, p. 213). The biracial young adult has developed the ability to perceive situations from more than one perspective.

Stephan and Stephan's Research of Ethnic Identity Among Mixed-Heritage Japanese American and Hispanic College Students

Stephan and Stephan (1989) researched choice of ethnic identity as well as antecedents of identity choices of two college-age, mixed-heritage student samples. Participants in both samples were enrolled in lower-level psychology courses at their respective campuses. The major goal of the study was to determine if mixed-heritage individuals identify with a single ethnic group.

The 67 University of Hawaii undergraduates were at least 25% but less than 100% Japanese and had a mean age of 19.7 years. The other ethnicities of the University of Hawaii students were Chinese, Caucasian, Hawaiian, Filipino, Portuguese, Korean, Okinawan, or Hispanic. The 104 part-Hispanic students at New Mexico State University had a mean age of 19.5 years. The other ethnicities of the New Mexico State University students were Caucasian, Native American Indian, or Black. Participants responded to questions addressing their choice of ethnic identity in five different settings.

In summarizing the results of the research, the authors stated that "contrary to the hypotheses of both assimilationist and pluralists, mixed-heritage people commonly have multiple identities" (Stephan & Stephan, 1989, p. 515). Because none of the participants consistently used a single mixed-heritage identity, the authors speculated that situations influence when these individuals choose to identify with their multiple heritages. Stephan and Stephan also suggested that ethnic boundaries may be fading inasmuch as so many of their mixed-heritage participants identified as having a multiple identity on one or more of the identity measures. The powerful influence of socializing children into the culture of the group as a factor in preserving a separate identity was recognized, but no common set of influential variables was found from the two investigations.

Alipuria's Research on College-Age Biracial Individuals

Alipuria's 1990 Master of Arts thesis at California State University, Los Angeles, gives us perspectives on college-age biracial individuals between the ages of 17 and 24. Alipuria's thesis is entitled, "Self Esteem and Self Label in Multiethnic Students from Two Southern California State Universities."

Students participating in Alipuria's research were enrolled in required general education classes at two campuses in the Los Angeles-Orange Counties area. The campuses differed in ethnic composition of students. For the sake of clarification, Alipuria labeled the campuses as the "ethnically diverse" campus and the "predominantly White" campus. On the ethnically diverse campus, White students were in the minority. On the predominantly White campus, two thirds of the students were White, and Hispanics made up the only sizable minority group. When the samples were combined for the two campuses, 9.0% of the students were multiethnic. Hispanic/White students made up 53.2% of the total sample of multiethnic students studied on both campuses. The other students participating had parents who were different combinations of Mexican American, White, Black, Asian, Native American, and multiethnic.

Alipuria's research investigated three hypotheses related to the self-esteem and self-label of the multiethnic students. The ethnic self-label came from the students' responses to the question: "If I am asked what is my ethnic group membership, I am most likely to say that I am: _____ " (Alipuria, 1990, pp. 44–45). In addition, students furnished answers to the sentences requesting the ethnic group belonged to by both their father and their mother. In cases where the self-label was unclear, the additional information on parental heritage helped to clarify whether the student was multiethnic.

In answer to the question on what students called themselves when asked about their ethnicity, "only about 20% of the subjects gave a response which unequivocally indicated a dual heritage" (Alipuria, 1990, p. 50). On the two campuses, a monoracial self-label was used by about three fourths of the students.

On the predominantly White campus, multiethnic students with one White parent were significantly more likely to identify themselves as White than multiethnic students with one White parent on the ethnically diverse campus. This confirmed Hypothesis A, "Students with one White parent will call themselves 'White' more often on the predominantly White campus than those on the ethnically diverse campus" (Alipuria, 1990, p. 40). On the ethnically diverse campus, multiethnic students with one White parent were significantly more likely to identify themselves with a non-White self-label.

The Rosenberg Self-Esteem Inventory was adapted to the format of a questionnaire. Results confirmed Hypothesis B "that there was no difference, statistically, in the self-esteem mean scores of multiethnic subjects from the highest scoring monoethnic group" (Alipuria, 1990, p. 53). The scores on self-esteem obtained by the multiethnic students were as high as the highest scores of their monoethnic peers.

The third hypothesis, Hypothesis C, that students who volunteer a multiethnic self-label will have higher self-esteem scores than the students who volunteer a monoethnic self-label, was not supported. No significant differences in self-esteem were found between the group volunteering a multiethnic self-label and the group volunteering a monoethnic self-label.

In discussion of implications from the investigation, Alipuria (1990) noted the following. First, when attempting to determine who is multiethnic, it may be important to ask more than the question of how the individual labels self. Since many participants in her research did not volunteer a multiethnic self-label, it would seem wise to ask also for ethnicity of both parents. Combining the responses to these questions would give a more accurate picture of which individuals are in reality multiethnic than simply asking the individual to give a self-label. Alipuria also noted that in completing routine forms indicating ethnicity, many multiethnic persons have the opportunity to choose only a monoethnic identity. The options on these forms need to be changed for multiethnic persons to get in the habit of declaring that they have more than one ethnic heritage.

Because more multiethnic students with White heritage identified themselves as White on the predominantly White campus than on the ethnically diverse campus, Alipuria wondered if this was an example of "situational ethnicity." It is possible that "the ability to fit in to the situation at hand may be the dynamic operating in the different patterns of self-label on the ethnically different campuses" (Alipuria, 1990, p. 63). Readers may note that "situational" ethnic identity choice also occurred in responses to the research of Stephan and Stephan (1989) on the two college campuses.

The findings of positive self-esteem of the multiethnic students on both of the campuses in Alipuria's research are significant. Several of the authors already cited in this book have expressed concerns about the marginal status of multiethnic people. This persistent negative image of people of interracial heritage is not supported by the results of this research. Readers will note that this is the third research report on multiethnic adolescents presented in this chapter that repudiates the negative marginal image of multiethnic or interracial adolescents.

The last area investigated by Alipuria was whether the individuals volunteering a multiethnic self-label would show higher self-esteem than individuals who volunteered a monoethnic self-label. Self-esteem for students volunteering a multiethnic self-label was not higher than self-esteem for students identifying as monoethnic.

A final area discussed by Alipuria is that of the importance of the community in developing a sense of identity. Alipuria (1990) asks: "Can the multiracial people develop a unique syncretic culture which is celebrated and passed on?" (p. 69). This new culture could provide the role models, support groups, and an ethnic reference group for the interracial people who often feel that no one completely understands them.

Research of Phinney and Associates

In Chapter 2 reference was made to the adolescent ethnic identity model of Jean Phinney (1989, 1993). Phinney's model is based on years of work in exploring many aspects of ethnic identity development of young people. Erikson's perspectives on adolescent identity development (Erikson, 1950, 1963, 1968), Marcia's model of four ego identity statuses (Marcia, 1966, 1980), and Tajfel's concepts on social identity theory (Tajfel, 1970, 1982) form the theoretical basis for Phinney's adolescent ethnic identity model. Phinney and Rosenthal (1992) note that "What is clear is that the child brings to adolescence a view of his or her ethnic heritage that has been shaped largely by family influences" (p. 152). Phinney's model concentrates heavily on the process of ethnic identity development in adolescence.

Phinney and her associates laid groundwork for her 1993 ethnic identity model through research of these groups of American-born high school and college students:

1. interviews with White and Black eighth graders to investigate their interest in and exploration of their ethnic identities (Phinney & Tarver, 1988);

2. interviews and assessment of tenth-grade Mexican American, Asian American, Black, and White students to examine their (a) extent of exploration of ethnic identity, (b) ego identity development, (c) levels of psychological functioning, and (d) self-concepts (Phinney, 1989);

3. a survey of Hispanic, Asian American, White, and Black college students to (a) learn how much they had explored their ethnic identities and (b) determine the relative importance of ethnicity as a reference group identity for these college students (Phinney & Alipuria, 1990);

4. a 3-year follow-up of the earlier study of tenth graders (Phinney & Chavira, 1992); and

5. the research of college and high school students of Hispanic, Asian, Black, White, and mixed heritage that served as the population to validate the Multigroup Ethnic Identity Measure (MEIM) (Phinney, 1992).

Phinney (1993) presents this three-stage model of adolescent ethnic identity:

Stage 1: Unexamined ethnic identity. In this stage the young persons have not spent time thinking about their ethnicity. Two possible substages of Stage 1 are the *diffuse* stage in which adolescents show no interest in their ethnic heritage or the *foreclosed* stage in which adolescents profess views on ethnicity that are not their own but are the views of significant others in their lives.

Stage 2: Ethnic identity search/moratorium. The adolescents in this stage are busy with investigations of their ethnic heritages. They are actively researching issues related to ethnicity and to the meaning of ethnicity in their lives. At this point, these young people are not yet ready to choose an ethnic identity as their own.

Stage 3: Achieved ethnic identity. The adolescents at this stage have reached a stage of clarity and confidence about their ethnic identities. They are willing to profess and cherish their ethnic heritage(s) and to tell what ethnicity means to them.

Phinney and her associates (Phinney, 1989; Phinney & Alipuria, 1990; Phinney & Rosenthal, 1992) propose that adolescents who attain an achieved ethnic identity (Stage 3) will feel positive about themselves. Phinney, Lochner, and Murphy (1990) suggest that committing to an ethnic identity is a critical factor in helping minority youth mediate negative influences of minority group status. Phinney and Rosenthal (1992) found that "links between self-esteem, ethnicity, and ethnic identity are not straightforward. . . . [and point to] the need to go beyond simple correlations between ethnic identity and self-esteem, if we are to 'unpackage' the true combinations of ethnic identity to well being" (p. 165).

A research report on how Hispanic adolescents between the ages of 16 and 19 deal with ethnicity and minority status (Chavira & Phinney, 1991) provides implications for counselor and teacher assistance in helping young people deal with stereotypes, discrimination, and membership in two cultures. The 26 Hispanic adolescents participating completed questionnaires measuring self-esteem, the Multigroup Ethnic Identity Measure (MEIM) (Phinney, 1992), and took part in in-depth interviews to explore their experiences with discrimination and stereotypes. The four strategies for dealing with discrimination were identified as: *assert*, show self-confidence or pride in one's group; *discuss*, explain how the stereotype is inaccurate or wrong; *disprove*, prove that the negative images are wrong; and *ignore*, show no outward response.

Participants who scored high on ethnic identity had significantly higher self-esteem than the subjects who scored low on ethnic identity, but self-esteem was not related to the way the adolescents dealt with discrimination and stereotypes. More than three fourths of the young people had experienced discrimination and nearly nine tenths of them thought that society holds negative stereotypes of Hispanics. Discussion was the most frequently reported strategy for dealing with discrimination and disproving was the most frequently reported strategy for dealing with stereotypes. Low ethnic identity adolescents reported using ignoring much more frequently than high ethnic identity youth in dealing with discrimination or stereotypes. The authors conclude: "The results are consistent with social identity theory, which suggests that having a clear opinion on active strategies for dealing with threats, rather than ignoring them, may contribute to the high self-esteem of high ethnic identity adolescents" (Chavira & Phinney, 1991, p. 227).

Readers interested in more details on Phinney's model of adolescent ethnic identity development are referred to the several sources cited and to Wehrly (1995). Information on the application of Phinney's model of adolescent ethnic identity development to interracial youth is discussed in the next section of this chapter.

Counselor Roles in Work With Interracial Adolescents

Counselors can work directly with interracial adolescents on an individual or small-group basis. Counselors can also influence students through working cooperatively with administrators and teachers to foster school climates that celebrate diversity. In order to have an impact on the total environment for the interracial high school or college student, a variety of roles are recommended for the counselor. Several of the activities described in the section Counselor Roles in Work With School Personnel in Chapter 4 are intervention strategies to promote a multicultural environment in the educational setting and can be modified for use with adolescents of high school or college ages.

A case example of an interracial secondary school student, Rose, is presented first. Following this, counselor roles are discussed along with appropriate interventions to assist Rose.

CASE EXAMPLE

Rose is an interracial 10th grader whose father is African American and whose mother is of Mexican American and Navajo heritage. Rose attends Cortez High in a southwest U.S. city. She has been referred to the 10th-grade counselor, Mr. Wood, for fighting in the halls and for low achievement.

Rose's school records indicate that she was a strong "B" student until her grades began to drop in the ninth grade. She has lived in the same city since she entered kindergarten. The schools that she has attended have been integrated with students of White, Mexican American, African American, Native American, and Asian American heritage. The largest group of students in her classes have been those of Mexican American and Native American Navajo descent. There are at least eight other high school students with more than one racial heritage at Cortez High School.

In the first conference with her counselor, Rose tells Mr. Wood that she feels pulled by different friendship cliques to declare her loyalty to one of them. They have told her that she has to decide what she is, either Black, Mexican American, or Native American Navajo Nation. Rose states that she is proud of all three of her heritages and wants to be able to claim all of them.

Rose is quite dark skinned and she tells Mr. Wood that most of the kids tell her she is Black and should associate with the Black friendship clique. Rose also talks about the prejudice she sometimes feels from the Mexican American group because her skin is so dark. Some of the Navajo students told her she could not possibly be Navajo because of her curly hair. She got in a fight before school because of teasing about her different appearance.

Rose agrees to see Mr. Wood on a weekly basis to work on resolving her problems. After Rose leaves his office, Mr. Wood realizes it is time to put into practice some things he learned in a summer school workshop on cross-cultural counseling with interracial adolescents.

Counselor Roles With School Administrators

School administrators play a leading role in determining the climate of acceptance of all people in their schools. Mr. Wood will continue to work with his administrators to help set a climate that promotes acceptance of diversity within Cortez High School.

One issue mentioned by numerous authors and by interracial individuals is the lack of opportunity for biracial/interracial people to indicate their total racial identity status on questionnaires, enrollment, and college admission forms. When asked to "Check One" for their race, interracial adolescents are forced to deny part of their racial heritage. Mr. Wood will work with school and college administrators to see that the options of "interracial," "mixed," or "multiracial" are added on enrollment and college admission forms and on any questionnaires that ask the student's race. As recommended by Alipuria (1990) the forms will also ask the racial background of both parents so the school can get an accurate picture of the number of interracial students.

Another change agent role for Mr. Wood is to serve on the curriculum review committee. Students of color and interracial students often have difficulty feeling that the curriculum is relevant to them. Mr. Wood will ask the committee to review the American history texts to see if they are limited to the White majority perspective on the history of the United States. To ensure that perspectives representing the diversity of contemporary U.S. society are included, the curricula of the arts and American literature are other areas that the curriculum committee may need to review.

Hatcher (1987) recommends exposing interracial adolescents "to academic material which allows them to understand the historical and cultural antecedents of diverse genetic backgrounds" (p. 204). Walton (1987) notes the need to monitor textbooks for covert teaching of prejudice. McCormick (1990) points to the need to promote nonsexist education. Mr. Wood can work with administrators and faculty members to build curricula that are relevant to all adolescents at Cortez High School.

Counselor Roles With Teachers

Mr. Wood will work actively with the faculty and staff in his school to magnify his support of multiculturalism and diversity through direct or indirect work with his teachers on classroom projects or investigations. A few of many topics appropriate for classroom use with adolescents are reviewed in this section. In one way or another all of the topics presented are related to the adolescent's search for identity. Mr. Wood will recommend that all students in a group or class participate in the activities suggested to eliminate the singling out of interracial young people as different.

A topic that could benefit all students is study of their racial/ethnic heritages. In the "Idea Exchange" section of the Spring 1995 issue of *Teaching Tolerance*, Kathy Gonzalez gives details on integrating student study of racial/ethnic heritages in an 11th-grade American literature class in San Jose, California. The family research project was done as preparation for reading *East of Eden* and was based on the theme "Generations." In cooperation with a computer science class in which the students were also enrolled, students constructed family trees to show three generations of their immediate families. Mr. Wood hopes to generate interest in a similar project for 10th graders at Cortez High School.

Research for the project will include interviewing at least three family members and consulting at least two written sources. The written sources can include family documents, books, newspapers, and encyclopedias. First-person accounts, including dialogue from their interviews, will be required in the final paper for the project. Sharing of stories about their families will occur as students review and edit each other's drafts.

Gonzalez reported that the assignment reaped many benefits. "Family and personal pride shone through in the students' writing, and many expressed their gratitude for having learned their family history so they could pass it on to their child" (Gonzalez, 1995, p. 8). These students of European, African, Asian, and Latino heritages found common ground in family rituals such as birthday and holiday celebrations. For many students, the project also fostered a new respect for the past. Mr. Wood anticipates that students at Cortez High School will also benefit greatly from the investigation.

Because interracial students are in the Cortez High School classes, Mr. Wood will recommend increasing the required interviews so that the interracial students will talk with at least two members of each of the family's interracial heritage. Other guidelines for this type of exploratory self-study are included in the section in Chapter 3 entitled Counselor Self-Study of Ethnic/Racial Heritage. One of the books suggested in Chapter 4, *Do People Grow on Family Trees?*

Genealogy for Kids & Other Beginners (Wolfman, 1991) is appropriate also for use with adolescents.

Mr. Wood will help teachers realize that student participation in study of their racial/ethnic heritage includes learning and applying many transferable skills. Interviewing skills are taught to gain family history information from older family members. Wolfman's (1991) book includes descriptions of this type of interviewing.

Research skills are honed through teaching methods to obtain family history. Students can learn to explore genealogical records in a variety of places, such as family attics (with trunks that contain family letters and photo albums), county courthouses, local libraries and museums, and the National Archives. A few students might eventually have the good fortune to travel to the homeland of their ancestors to learn more about family history.

Mr. Wood will also work with teachers to encourage use of multicultural literature. Rochman's (1993) *Against Borders: Promoting Books for a Multicultural World* contains annotations and a wealth of suggestions for use of literature that helps to expand world views of junior and senior high students. Johnson and Smith's *Dealing with Diversity Through Multicultural Fiction—Library-Classroom Partnerships* (1993) outlines an interdisciplinary curriculum for young adolescents that integrates books that address a variety of diversity issues (ethnicity, race, culture, gender, generation, age, family structure, and disabilities). Many of the nearly 1,000 multicultural and international book annotations in Miller-Lachmann's *Our Family, Our Friends, Our World* (1992) described in Chapter 4 are books appropriate for teenagers.

Books with interracial adolescents as important characters are listed in Appendix B. Appropriate books may be selected for classroom discussions from the framework of bibliotherapy discussed in Chapters 3 and 4. Small- and large-group discussions of books can promote acquisition of information and expansion of critical thinking skills.

Mr. Wood will also work with teachers on units and discussions of prejudice, stereotyping, discrimination, and racism (Ponterotto, 1991; Ponterotto & Pedersen, 1993; Walton, 1987). Students will be encouraged to consider the four strategies for dealing with discrimination that were researched by Chavira and Phinney (1991): assert, discuss, disprove, and ignore.

There are many materials that Mr. Wood and the teachers can review for planning and implementing activities on prejudice reduction and improvement of race relations. Sherman (1990) described school counselor involvement in planning and helping to deliver a curriculum "that attempts to deal openly with the issues of prejudice and intergroup conflict" (p. 17).

Ponterotto (1991) delineated the Flight or Fight Response Theory of Racial Stress that integrated concepts from Allport's seminal work, *The Nature of Prejudice* (1954), and from Helms's (1990) White racial identity development theory. Ponterotto also outlined interventions to promote positive identity development for White students and those of color. Three emphases were discussed that applied to all developmental levels:

1. Multicultural and nonsexist education from preschool through college years is a prerequisite to establishing an accepting and tolerant society.
2. Qualitative interracial contact occurs under these four conditions: (a) equal status between the individuals of different racial heritages, (b) enough contact to dispel stereotypes about the groups represented, (c) contact in which the individuals work together to achieve goals, and (d) a context in which the social norms favor the various groups equally.
3. Individuals' attitudes must be addressed in order to combat the roots of prejudice. Ponterotto (1991) noted that "Prejudicial attitudes make for selective memory" (p. 221).

Ponterotto (1991) suggested the use of popular literature, contemporary fiction, and media in designing secondary school programs that combat the roots of prejudice. At the college level he recommended the continued use of films and literature to stimulate both same-race and interethnic group discussions to promote multicultural understanding. Ponterotto and Pedersen's 1993 book, *Preventing Prejudice: A Guide for Counselors and Educators*, provides a theoretical base for prejudice prevention as well as a variety of group exercises for operationalizing these programs.

Teaching Tolerance, the previously cited magazine published by the Southern Poverty Law Center (SPLC), contains ideas for use with high school students as well as with elementary children. SPLC is also producing curriculum materials (including videos and detailed lesson plans) on tolerance topics. The first of these kits, *America's Civil Rights Movement*, was made available in late 1991. Since that time over 50,000 of these kits have been distributed free to schools around the country (Staff, 1994, December 1). "A Time for Justice," the video component of *America's Civil Rights Movement*, was awarded the Oscar in the 1995 Academy of Motion Picture Arts and Sciences short documentary category competition. The documentary film, *The Shadow of Hate: A History of Intolerance in America*, and the accompanying publication *Us and Them: A History of Intolerance in America* (Carnes, 1995) were released for free classroom use by SPLC in Spring 1995. Readers can learn of the availability of the teaching kits by writing to *Teaching Tolerance*, the Southern Poverty Law Center, 400 Washington Avenue, Montgomery, Alabama 36104.

Assessment of Mental Health of Interracial Adolescents

An important task for Mr. Wood in counseling with Rose will be the assessment of her mental health. First, Mr. Wood will need to determine if the problems brought by Rose are associated with her interracial status (Gibbs, 1989). As noted earlier, it is dangerous for clinicians to assume that all behavioral or psychological problems brought by interracial adolescents are related to ethnic identity development conflicts.

Gibbs (1989) states that the central and first issue to assess in work with biracial adolescents is their underlying attitudes toward having more than one racial heritage. Adolescents must integrate their dual or multiple heritages before they can work on other developmental tasks of identity achievement. Mr. Wood will need to determine if and how well Rose has resolved conflicts related to:

(a) her multiple racial/ethnic identity, (b) social marginality, (c) sexuality, (d) autonomy, and (e) educational and occupational aspirations.

In assessment of defense mechanisms and coping strategies employed by Rose, Mr. Wood may detect anxiety, guilt, fear of social rejection, repression, regression, rejection of parental values, rationalization, projection, intellectualization, or identification with the aggressor. Gibbs (1989) identified three trends that may emerge in evaluating the wide spectrum of defense mechanisms and coping strategies employed by biracial Black-White adolescents in their search for a racial/ethnic identity. Even though Rose does not have White heritage, Mr. Wood may need to consider these three possibilities for Rose:

1. The biracial teens who have assumed a negative identity often show denial or acting out defense mechanisms and cope through maladaptive and socially dysfunctional behavior such as low school achievement and sexual promiscuity. Rose has already shown a decline in school achievement since entering the ninth grade.

2. The biracial teens who have adopted a negative identity often identify with the most deviant and devalued stereotypes of their Black heritage. They behave in a manner to achieve a self-fulfilling prophecy of these negative stereotypes. Mr. Wood wonders if the fight that Rose engaged in might be indicative of this. Exploration of this possible issue will be ongoing in forthcoming counseling sessions.

3. The biracial teens who have overidentified with their White heritage will present a facade of adaptation to the majority culture, but this overidentification often exacts a high psychic cost. These are the young people who may seem emotionally and sexually inhibited, overly close to their families, and show perfectionistic behavior (Gibbs, 1989). Inasmuch as Rose has no White heritage, this may not be a part of her problem. However, overidentification with any one of her ethnic heritages could result in a high psychic cost to Rose.

Gibbs (1987, 1989) suggested other general areas of assessment of biracial Black-White adolescents that seem to have applicability to the case of Rose:

1. *Behaviors and concerns that are developmentally age-appropriate and that do not indicate identity conflicts and problems.* A great variety of behaviors and concerns such as peer relationships, fluctuations in

school performance, mood shifts, or minor family rebelliousness may surface during adolescence and are not ordinarily indicators of severe pathology. Mr. Wood will explore how much Rose's decline in school performance and problems with peer relationships may be related to her interracial identity development.

If Rose displays more severe behavioral or psychological problems, they will need to be evaluated for successful ethnic identity achievement rather than identity diffusion (showing no interest in ethnic identity), foreclosure (letting others [like parents or peers] decide one's ethnic identity), or adoption of a negative ethnic identity (taking on the most devalued traits of one's ethnic heritage). Undersocialization will manifest itself in antisocial, impulsive, or alienated behaviors. Oversocialization may result in overconforming, constricted, or overachieving behaviors.

2. *Parental and family attitudes.* It will be important for Mr. Wood to assess if Rose's parents or other family members are giving her conflicting messages about her multiple heritage. White parents sometimes adopt any of these three attitudes toward their Black-White adolescent offspring: (a) show denial, (b) give mixed messages, or (c) act as if all of society is "color blind." Rose's parents are not White, but they may still show denial or give mixed messages. Details on work with the interracial family are included in Chapter 7, Counseling Interracial Families.

3. *Resources of the school and community.* Mr. Wood has already examined the racial/ethnic composition and balance of the student body of Cortez High School as well as that of the faculty and staff. Community resources to help Rose and her family develop positive feelings about themselves will be explored. Mr. Wood will also search out answers to these questions: Are the interracial adolescents and their families welcome in area churches, recreational facilities, and shopping areas? Is there an active interracial support group in the immediate area? If the support does not exist, what is being done to change this?

4. *Social networks and peer relationships.* Mr. Wood may search for answers to these questions: How do the social networks function in integration of interracial teens like Rose? Are Rose and the other interracial adolescents accepted as normal teenagers or are they scape-

goated to gain acceptance in clubs or groups? It will be important for Mr. Wood to gain additional perspectives from Rose regarding her perceptions of relationships with her peers. Discussion of this for several sessions may be necessary for Rose and Mr. Wood to gain a wider picture of Rose's interpersonal peer relationships. This may also be an area for group work with the interracial teens at Cortez High School. Actions taken should be something with which the teens concur and with which the teens will feel comfortable.

General Guidelines for Counseling With Interracial Adolescents

Several guidelines are outlined for the counselor who works with interracial adolescents by Gibbs (1987, 1989) and Overmier (1990). Although these guidelines are discussed separately from assessment of the mental health of interracial adolescents, much of the process of assessment occurs during the counseling sessions.

The first task for Mr. Wood is to establish a working relationship with Rose. In Chapter 3, the challenge of establishing a cross-cultural relationship was discussed as were guidelines for cross-cultural counseling. Counseling will not be productive until a working relationship has been established between the counselor and the counselee.

A second counseling recommendation is to give Rose the opportunity to ventilate feelings. These feelings need to be validated as rational by Mr. Wood in a nonjudgmental manner. It is at this point that Mr. Wood's comfort with listening to the feelings of Rose will be especially evident. Mr. Wood's cognizance of the social realities for Rose and other interracial people will also surface in responses to Rose.

A third guideline stresses the important role that the counselor plays in helping to support and build the self-esteem of interracial clients like Rose. Counselors encourage interracial clients to describe and develop their abilities, their interests, and their positive coping mechanisms. Work may be needed to determine if the interests and coping mechanisms are ones chosen by Rose or adopted because she believes these behaviors are expected of her. Helping Rose to plan, try out, and adopt new behaviors may be ongoing for several sessions.

A fourth area that may need Mr. Wood's attention is that of confusion that Rose may manifest. Sometimes this confusion is linked to confusion over racial identity. Details on maladaptive ethnic identity development are described in a previous section, Assessment of Mental Health of Interracial Adolescents. Mr. Wood can help Rose look at her behavior and decide if she needs to develop more productive racial/ethnic identity paths.

An additional area for Mr. Wood to examine with Rose is how much she has explored all sides of her racial heritage. If she gets involved in classroom projects to study her racial heritages (as described in a previous section of this chapter), she will probably have a good start on this process. Activities described for classroom projects can be adapted for individual work with Rose if she has not engaged in this study. Or, if Rose has already done some exploration of her family heritage, she may be interested in additional work in this area. Mr. Wood can play an important role in listening to and encouraging Rose's family heritage exploration.

Counselors should be involved with the families of interracial adolescents so that the young people will not feel singled out as the family problem. Details on work with interracial families are included in Chapter 7, Counseling Interracial Families.

Another important role for Mr. Wood is to facilitate a support group (or groups) for the interracial teens at Cortez High School (Alipura, 1990; Funderburg, 1994; Gibbs, 1987). Support groups provide the opportunity for interracial adolescents to meet with others who face similar challenges and dilemmas. The young people feel less alone when they realize that others are like them in facing the issues of more than one racial heritage. Sharing ideas on how to meet dilemmas faced by other interracial teens can provide hope and encouragement for Rose. An important goal of interracial support groups is that of helping these adolescents develop pride in being different. Ideally, the support group leader or co-facilitator will be of interracial heritage. Mr. Wood hopes to identify an interracial person who can work with him in facilitating these support groups.

Several authors have recognized that interracial youth often identify themselves racially according to the group they are with (Alipuria, 1990; Brown, 1995; Root, 1990, 1994; Stephan & Stephan,

1989). Discussion of the appropriateness of situational racial self-identification should be included in counseling with Rose.

Based on previous studies that found that adolescents with an achieved identity showed higher levels of psychological functioning (Phinney, 1989) and higher self-esteem (Phinney & Alipuria, 1990), the authors recommend that counselors work with minority youth on several issues: (a) exploration of feelings related to their ethnicity, (b) learning about the history of their group within a multicultural society, and (c) discussing ways to live biculturally or multiculturally. Mr. Wood will explore these issues with Rose in individual sessions and assess the readiness of Rose to work in small groups. Group sessions can be especially productive in helping interracial youth like Rose dispel negative images that they may have of their racial status. Phinney et al. (1990) warned that although these discussions can sometimes "invoke a somewhat disturbing exploration or moratorium period, the process can be expected to lead ultimately to a more secure sense of self and more healthy adjustment" (p. 68).

Special Considerations for Counseling Interracial Adolescents in Foster or Adoptive Homes

Interracial Adolescents in Foster Homes

In Chapter 4, I noted the paucity of literature on counseling interracial children in foster home care. The same situation exists for literature on counseling interracial adolescents in foster homes. These older youth face many of the same issues discussed in the section Special Considerations for Counseling Interracial Children in Foster Homes in Chapter 4.

Intense feelings of insecurity and rejection are experienced by some of these adolescents as a result of being moved from one foster home to another. Their interracial status can put them in the "double jeopardy" of not knowing where they fit racially nor where they fit in the societal structure (because they have never known a permanent home that they can call their own).

It may be necessary for the counselor to engage these interracial adolescents in extensive discussions of their problems to determine, first, how the young people perceive their problems, and, second, to "sort out" issues on which the adolescents wish to work. Guidelines for assessment of mental health of interracial adolescents presented earlier in this chapter are applicable. Counselor-led, small-group sessions with other interracial youth in foster care can provide a forum for developing a support group to vent feelings, discuss problems, and share alternatives for change. Mr. Wood will plan special sessions for the interracial youth at Cortez High School who are in foster home care.

Interracial Adolescents in Adoptive Homes

Most of the scant literature on adopted interracial adolescents has been written by social workers or social psychologists studying the phenomena of inracial or transracial adoption. A 1983 book by McRoy and Zurcher, *Transracial and Inracial Adoptees: The Adolescent Years*, provides data from their extensive study of these two types of adoptions. Interracial Black-White adolescents and adolescents with two Black parents were included in their research. All adolescents in the study were categorized as Black. The adoption of interracial adolescents by White parents was considered transracial, but the adoption of interracial adolescents by Black parents was considered inracial. (Note the automatic categorization of these biracial youth as Black.)

It is significant to note that no statistical difference was found on self-esteem between transracially adopted and inracially adopted adolescents in the McRoy and Zurcher (1983) study. All of these adolescents had quite normative levels of self-esteem.

Although the study was done several years ago, there are implications from the research that Mr. Wood may want to pursue for interracial adopted adolescents in his school. One finding was that interracial youth seemed more reluctant to discuss racist incidents with White adopted parents (transracial adoptions) than with Black adopted parents (inracial adoptions). Mr. Wood could find it productive to explore racist incidents experienced by Cortez High School interracial young people adopted by White parents.

A second implication for counselor intervention came from the finding that the transracially adopted youth had teachers who expected more of them because they had White parents than these teachers expected of the interracial youth placed in Black homes. Some of the transracial adoptees also reported that they believed that their teachers were more helpful to them and more willing to talk to their White parents than to the Black parents. The self-fulfilling prophecy can come into play in such a situation. Mr. Wood can investigate the possibility of this happening at Cortez High School and work to help teachers change how they relate and interact with interracial young people and their adoptive parents so that all young people reach their potential.

A third finding was that more attention to pride in being Black was occurring for the adoptees in the homes where both parents were Black than in the transracial homes with White parents. McRoy and Zurcher (1983) were concerned that the interracial youth in White homes might not be receiving socialization "to become bicultural and to realistically perceive the historical and current black-white relations in American society" (p. 140). Another implication of this finding is that the interracial youth in both White and Black homes may now need help in developing pride in their dual identities with the recent emphasis on allowing interracial people to decide their own ethnic identity. Given the recent findings of the importance of adolescent development of positive feelings about ethnic identity and its possible impact on overall psychological functioning, it will be important for counselors to monitor the ethnic identity development of transracial adoptees.

The results of more current research on transracial adoption are included in *The Case for Transracial Adoption* by Simon, Alstein, and Melli (1994). This book reviews the Simon-Alstein 20 years of longitudinal research with transracially adopted children, their families, and their communities. This empirical research investigated whether transracial adoption is in the best interest of the child and presented a positive picture for adoption across races. Recommendations from Simon et al. (1994) are included in Chapter 7.

Counselors interested in a recent account of the adoption of a Black-White interracial daughter and an African American daughter into a White family with two young sons may find Bates's (1993) *Gift Children: A Story of Race, Family, and Adoption in a Divided America* enlightening. The story covers 23 years in the life of the Bates family and describes in detail the difficulties that the family faced when the adopted daughters became adolescents.

Summary

Counseling roles with interracial adolescents have been the focus of Chapter 5. After an introduction to the magnitude of the interracial adolescent's task of integrating all of her or his racial heritages into a positive identity, the chapter reiterated the need for counselor self-awareness as the first step in counseling these unique young people. Issues faced by interracial adolescents centered on the need to redefine relationships while choosing an ethnic identity in the contemporary racist society.

Recent research on the racial/cultural/ethnic identity of interracial adolescents was reviewed. Results of three major studies (Alipuria, 1990; Gibbs & Hines, 1992; Kerwin et al., 1993) presented a positive picture of interracial adolescent identity development. Stephan and Stephan (1989) found that a high percentage of mixed-heritage undergraduates on two campuses identified themselves as having a multiple identity on at least one or more identity measures and that situations may determine what identity is chosen. Phinney's model of adolescent identity development was also introduced as applicable for use with the interracial population.

Counselor roles for both direct and indirect service to interracial adolescents were described as they related to the hypothetical case of Rose, an interracial sophomore in the U.S. southwest. Heavy involvement in work with the significant others of teens like Rose was recommended. Procedures for assessment of the mental health of interracial adolescents and guidelines for counseling were delineated. A closing section addressed the special needs of interracial youth in foster homes and in adoptive homes.

6

Counseling
Interracial Adults

Attaining adulthood does not necessarily mean the interracial individual no longer faces problems related to having more than one racial heritage. Many interracial adults continue to deal with issues of their heritage throughout their lifetimes.

This chapter addresses counseling roles with interracial adults. Topics are addressed under these headings: Counselor Self-Awareness as the First Step in Counseling Interracial Adults, Issues Faced by Interracial Adults, Contemporary Perspectives on the Racial/Cultural/Ethnic/Identity Development of Interracial Adults, and Counselor Roles in Work With Interracial Adults.

Counselor Self-Awareness as the First Step in Counseling Interracial Adults

Root (1994) cautions counselors that "Therapy with multiracial people can prompt us to examine our assumptions about race and ethnicity and the degree to which we have internalized a pseudoscientific and oppressive belief system" (p. 474). Root also explains how a therapist with internalized oppressive belief systems about multiracial people might misdiagnose the problems brought by a multiracial client. These warnings support the need for counselors who work with interracial adults to engage in in-depth self-assessment of the attitudes, values, and beliefs they hold related to interracial individuals. The counselor is referred to the process for this self-examination outlined in Chapter 3 under the heading Counselor Self-Study of Ethnic/Racial Heritage.

Issues Faced by Interracial Adults

The development of an appropriate identification with one's ethnic, cultural, and racial heritage(s) is a developmental task of childhood and adolescence. For the child and the adolescent with more than one racial heritage, the process can be complex and difficult in a society permeated by prejudice and racism. When this developmental task is not achieved prior to adulthood, the resolution of identification with two or more racial backgrounds may become even more challenging. Unless the interracial individual seeks help in the development of a dual or multiracial identity, the person may be plagued by this unresolved issue throughout his or her lifetime.

Unresolved memories of feeling different and devalued, of experiencing rejection and loneliness, and of dealing with guilt over rejecting part (or all) of one's racial heritage may surface in counseling with interracial adults. In addition, these adult clients may ask counselors to help them deal with ongoing questions and comments about their "differentness."

Contemporary Perspectives on the Racial/Cultural/Ethnic Identity Development of Interracial Adults

As noted in Chapter 2, research on racial/ethnic identity development of interracial adults is of relatively recent origin. Since the early 1980s several U.S. doctoral dissertations have investigated the identity issues of these adults. Many of the adults participating shared memories of phases and stages that they experienced as interracial children and adolescents. Descriptive information from these retrospective reports is included in this chapter because counselors working with interracial adults may hear their clients describe memories of similar painful childhood and adolescent experiences. These memories can provide clues for work on issues of unfinished racial/ethnic identity development. An overview of each of these empirical studies follows.

Hall's Perspectives on Black-Japanese Biracial Identity

In 1980 and 1992 Hall reported on her doctoral studies to determine how Black-Japanese identified themselves and the factors that led to this identification. The 30 subjects for her investigation were over the age of 18, had Black fathers and Japanese mothers, and were interviewed through a questionnaire designed by Hall that included a self-administered section and an interviewer-administered section. Two measures of self-esteem were included in the self-administered section.

Eighteen of the individuals self-identified as Black; 10 chose the "Other" category; 1 identified as Japanese; and 1 chose not to categorize himself racially. An ethnic identity choice regression to determine the relative influence of other variables on Black ethnic identity choice revealed "that those Black-Japanese who were young, had knowledge of the Black culture, had predominantly Black friends, and perceived nonacceptance by Japanese American peers tended to identify as Black" (Hall, 1992, p. 255). A regression analysis of responses of individuals who chose "Other Than Black" identity showed the opposite influence of other variables (were older, had less knowledge of Black culture, had fewer Black friends, and felt accepted by Japanese Americans).

No significant correlation was found between ethnic identity choice and self-esteem. No differences were found between sexes in their choice of ethnic identity. No effects of mother's generation were found between the offspring of the 24 first-generation immigrant mothers (Issei) and offspring of the 6 second-generation mothers (Nisei).

Ethnicity of neighborhood and friends showed that a stronger identification with one's Black heritage occurred in neighborhoods that were predominantly Black. Choice of Black identity correlated at the .01 level of significance with both objective and subjective knowledge of Black culture. No significant correlations were found between fluency in either the Japanese language or in Black English and ethnic identity choice. The only significant variable in political involvement was that biracial individuals involved in other movements such as the United Farm Workers chose an ethnic identity other than Black more often than those not involved in political movements.

Acceptance of Blacks by the respondents correlated significantly with Black identity, but acceptance of Japanese by the respondents was not significant with Japanese identity. Self-reports on racial resemblance indicated that most believed that they looked more Black than any other race.

Sixty percent of the respondents recalled a time in their lives when they felt that they had to make a decision about an ethnic identity. The decision-making periods began at ages 14 or 15 and lasted for 3 or 4 years. There was no correlation between experiencing this ethnic identity choice period and the choice of ethnic identity. Hall speculated that the ethnic decision process may have been an unconscious one for several of the participants because all seemed to be well adjusted and showed positive self-esteem scores.

Ninety-three percent of the respondents rated themselves high on "Blackness" while 87% rated themselves high on "Japaneseness." Hall interpreted this as an indication that her subjects viewed themselves as both biracial and bicultural.

When asked to list negative and positive aspects of being biracial, the participants gave positive comments two times as often as they made negative comments. The negative experiences were described as occurring more often during their childhood years. The positive comments mentioned most frequently by these Black-Japanese were inheriting the best qualities of both cultures; understanding, accepting, and empathizing with people who are of different races; being beautiful people with physical features from both races; having strong family units; and viewing their biracialism and biculturalism as strong assets.

Half of the participants indicated that they did not feel totally accepted by people of both of their heritages; Hall saw this as a marginal position for these 15 people. Because there are so few Black-Japanese, this group can be viewed as a minority within a minority. However, the overwhelming identification with both cultures was viewed as positive since respondents did not feel they had to fit into one racial mold.

Thornton's Social History of Black-Japanese Americans

A 1983 dissertation by Thornton combined a major review of historic and current literature on mixed-race individuals with findings from his in-depth study of 61 members of Black-Japanese American families in four geographic areas of the United States (Kansas, Washington, D.C., Massachusetts, and Michigan). The families consisted of African American fathers, Japanese mothers, and their offspring who were at least 18 years of age.

Ninety-one percent of the offspring of these interracial marriages, the Black-Japanese Americans (BJAs), had faced a racial identity crisis or choice-making period in their lives at about 13 years of age. For those growing up on military installations, the identity dilemma surfaced when they were with civilians or when their fathers retired from the military.

Of particular note were findings on how BJAs perceived they were viewed by the two groups of their racial heritage. Almost half felt they were disliked by both Blacks and Japanese. More than three fourths of the BJAs felt they had the most in common with other BJAs. About two thirds of the BJAs felt they had almost nothing in common with Blacks or with Japanese. When asked in what environment they felt most comfortable, about three fifths stated the White environment, about one fourth said they felt equally comfortable in a Japanese or White environment, and about one seventh chose a Black and Japanese environment; no one chose a Black environment alone.

In summarizing the in-depth discussions, Thornton found these four identities among the Black-Japanese adult sons and daughters:

1. *American* (14%)—BJAs who had little substantive knowledge of either heritage, no experience with a racial identity crisis, no beliefs that race is important, and little awareness of societal constraints.

2. *Biracials* (57%)—BJAs who had more knowledge of their cultural heritages than the American group, experienced an identity crisis that moved them from an external to an internal locus of control, a perspective that saw race as of slight importance, some understanding of social structure and social constraints, and perceptions that "blame the victim."

3. *Black* (14%)—BJAs who saw race as very important, worked at being Black and associated mainly with Black people, chose the Black identity after experiencing a racial identity crisis, and understood the marginality of Black Americans.

4. *Multiethnics* (15%)—BJAs who chose to continue efforts to understand all three parts of their heritage (Black, Japanese, and middle-class American), were knowledgeable about their African heritage, and were striving to learn more about their Japanese roots.

In analyzing professed racial attitudes and beliefs, Thornton underscored the complexity and multifaceted nature of responses of the BJA offspring. Even though few of them expressed "core" attitudes of a Black identity in their in-depth responses, when asked to apply a racial or ethnic label to themselves 51% identified as Black, 37% chose a biracial identity, and 12% selected a Japanese identity. "This lack of congruence between labels and the attitudes behind them is a significant concern to any 'racial' model of identity" (Thornton, 1983, p. 138).

In integrating findings from his own research of BJAs with a review of the literature on multiethnic/multiracial identity, Thornton (1983) listed these as important assumptions:

1. Multiethnic people should be viewed from a panoramic perspective that sees them as both active and passive in determining their ethnic identity.
2. Multiethnic identity is a process and not a static entity.
3. Racial identity shows itself in a subjective manner and varies from individual to individual.
4. "It is not constructive to consider race for BJAs in opposition, apposition may be better in the long run" (p. 177).
5. Core identity and role identity may differ. In the past research has tapped role identity.
6. "It is equally if not more important to know how boundaries are formed, why particular ones are chosen and how they are crossed or changed than it is to know the content of the boundaries (i.e., cultural differences). Past research has focused primarily on the latter" (pp. 177–178).

Kich's Stages of Japanese/White Biracial Identity Development

Kich's 1982 dissertation reported on his study of the influences of family, peers, and social factors on the ethnic/racial identity development of 15 biracial Japanese/White adults. Based on his earlier dissertation research on involvement with multiracial community groups and on experiences as a clinical psychologist with people of many different races, Kich (1992) presented his three-stage ethnic identity development model for all people of multiracial heritage.

Stage 1 is *Awareness of Differentness and Dissonance*. This stage is a painful one when the interracial child realizes that he or she is different and interprets this differentness negatively. It usually occurs between the ages of 3 and 10 when the child begins to associate with peer and reference groups outside of the home and gets the message that differentness is devalued. A devalued sense of self can follow.

Parents may be experiencing so much personal and societal stress in their biracial marriage that they (the parents) are unaware of the difficulties their children are experiencing. The families do not discuss racial identity issues or provide positive interracial labels for their children.

Movement into Stage 2, *Struggle for Acceptance*, occurs when the individual makes contact with supportive peer groups and begins feeling comfortable with interracial self-labels. The adolescent need for peer acceptance may heighten a feeling of separation between home and school. A struggle to identify with both parents often ensues at the same time that the interracial youth is struggling to separate from parents.

The divorce of the biracial individual's parents does not solve the question of loyalty. Reconciliation with the absent parent appears to be a necessary step toward continuing development of an interracial identity.

Changes in peer reference groups and in contacts with extended families during high school often result in rapid fluctuations in self-perceptions for interracial adolescents. There may be a "trying on" of various reference groups to feel accepted and avoid facing the ambiguities of being "both" and "neither." Acceptance by others outside of the home is paramount. "But, unlike others, biracial and bicultural people do not find an easy or comfortable recognition, acceptance, and membership with others like themselves" (Kich, 1992, p. 312).

Kich characterized Stage 3, *Self-Acceptance of an Interracial Identity*, as having these four components: (a) recognition of a dual racial heritage, (b) recognition of how self is alike and different from each of one's parents, (c) assertion of an interracial self-label, and (d) demonstration of a need for an interracial reference group. Reaching this third stage requires interracial individuals to develop a congruent and positive definition of self rather than merely accepting stereotyped definitions ascribed to them by others.

The stage of a stable interracial and intercultural self-identity usually begins after high school and continues while the person is in higher education or in occupational pursuits. Extended family contact is by choice and fulfills a need for a conscious link with part of self.

Interracial people at this stage become more self-confident and are able to choose when to fit in and when to confront distortions. The interpersonal skills associated with passing are used to gain acceptance from people of many different groups and to negotiate situations with rigid and limiting expectations. At this point many interracial individuals actively seek out other biracial, bicultural people and those of different ethnic and racial groups. Being able to accept and assert that they are biracial or interracial is an ongoing and unfinished lifelong process for these individuals.

Murphy-Shigematsu's Amerasian Research

In 1987 Murphy-Shigematsu reported on his study of how U.S. Amerasians between the ages of 23 and 33 attempted to resolve their racial identity issues and concerns. The qualitative research used in-depth, semistructured interviews with 10 Amerasian offspring of Japanese mothers and White American fathers. They grew to adulthood on the East Coast in non–Japanese American communities and attended East Coast colleges.

In the years of childhood and adolescence, participants recalled concerns from being in an intercultural, interracial, and international family. Themes that emerged were those of experiencing confusion and pain related to being different, feeling isolated, dealing with family issues, and feeling pressures to assimilate. Coping with differences in culture and race had occurred during very formative years and left indelible impressions.

The themes of resolution of these issues were those of definition, roots, community, and integration. The desire to learn about their bicultural heritages had a strong influence on their lives. The need to connect with others who were experiencing similar issues and struggles emerged. Resolution of the concerns and issues of these Amerasians involved defining, accepting, and asserting their unique racial and cultural self-images.

Anderson's Research of Ethnic Identity in Biracial Asian Americans

In 1993 Anderson studied major factors that influenced the ethnic identity of 48 biracial adults between the ages of 18 and 30 who had one Asian parent of Chinese, Japanese, or Korean descent and one White, European American parent. Most of the participants were recruited from campuses in the Los Angeles area. Participation was through completion of a mailed questionnaire.

Anderson's study was designed as correlational and nonexperimental research. In this research, the five predictor variables were Ethnic Composition of the Neighborhood, Support Networks, Cultural Exposure, Attitudes and Behaviors of the Asian Parent Regarding Race and Racial Issues, and Attitudes and Behaviors of the White Parent Regarding Race and Racial Issues. Ethnic Identity was the sole dependent variable in the research.

Anderson researched six main hypotheses and two secondary hypotheses. A significant positive correlation was found only between Cultural Exposure and Ethnic Identity. The main research hypothesis, that the five predictor variables as a group would significantly predict Ethnic Identity, was confirmed. Secondary hypotheses results indicated that the majority of Anderson's participants identified with both of their racial heritages in at least one of the contexts specified in the questionnaire, varied in the way they identified according to the situational contexts, and felt closest to other biracial Asian Americans rather than to Whites or Asian Americans.

Brown's Study of the Racial Self-Identification of Black/White Interracial Young Adults

Brown's 1991 dissertation researched "racial identity, conflict, self-esteem and experiential/physical factors in young adults with one black and one white parent" (p. 2116A). Included in her retrospective and cross-sectional study were 119 U.S.-born young adults between 18 and 35 years of age with one Black and one White parent.

Results of the research did not confirm that the racial identity development path for Black/White children is a linear journey toward Blackness. The racial identities chosen varied among participants and the process was multidimensional. Although some identified as Black and a few identified as White, the majority of the participants indicated they would identify as interracial if given the choice.

Differences in how they identified publicly and saw themselves privately also were reported. Brown saw this compartmentalization into public and private identities as a way to cope with societal pressures to disregard their White roots while holding fast to their interracial self-perceptions. Fluctuations in racial identity choices occurred as they went through the various developmental phases, but interracial identity choices increased as they grew older. Significant predictors of racial identity were social environmental experiences, contact with various racial groups, exposure to Black and White cultures, and physical appearance or phenotype. The majority of the participants (three fourths) had experienced some degree of racial identity conflict in their growing-up years.

All three identities (Black, White, interracial) have the potential for conflict. The interracial identity is not an officially legitimate one in the United States, but the Black or White identities each represent only half of the heritage of these people. Identifying as White is not a correct legal identification for interracial Black/White individuals. Three fifths of the respondents reported that they had successfully resolved their racial identity through realizing that their biracial background would not be recognized, through finding their public and private identities congruent, or through being public about their interracial self-perceptions. Brown noted that her research did not confirm that choosing the Black identity is the most successful resolution; the research did confirm, however, that there is a high emotional cost in choosing a White identity. "Only interracial identity was associated with significantly diminished conflict" (Brown, 1995, p. 129).

Brown noted that legal and social sanctions of the interracial heritage of people of mixed heritage would go far in reducing emotional turmoil they experience in declaring their racial identity. She also recognized the social and political implications of creating a new racial category that would diminish numbers of other people of color categories.

Wijeyesinghe's Research of Racial Self-Identification of African American/Euro-American Adults

Wijeyesinghe's 1992 dissertation examined "how a select group of adults of African-American/Euro-American heritage came to choose or develop a sense of racial identity" (p. 3808-A). Seven women and men whose ages ranged from 21 to 59 participated in in-depth phenomenological interviews to determine what influenced them to choose either a Black, White, or mixed racial identity; what their worlds had been like having chosen the specific racial identities; and what special meaning these identity choices had to each interviewee.

In-depth profiles were prepared for each participant from the interview transcripts. Themes emerged when profiles were compared across racial, gender, and age groups. The three factors that appeared to have the most influence on choice of racial identity were (a) present and past cultural affiliations, (b) early socialization experiences, and (c) physical appearance. Several other factors that had a lesser influence on racial identity choice were the extent and nature of involvement in individual political experiences, the kind of social values preeminent in a given period of history, the individual's biological racial heritage, and the "participant's sense of spirituality and connection to other social identities such as gender, religion, age, and ethnic identity" (Wijeyesinghe, 1992, p. 3808-A).

Participants' experiences were discussed within the framework of selected racial identity development models for Black, White, and biracial populations. The individual's awareness of his or her own race and racism as described in current models of racial identity development emerged as an additional factor for understanding the racial identity choices of the participants.

The Adulthood Stage of the Kerwin-Ponterotto Model of Biracial Identity Development

Kerwin and Ponterotto (1995) view the development of a biracial identity as a lifelong process. Biracial individuals move into the Adulthood Stage after successful resolution of the challenges of the first five stages: Preschool, Entry to School, Preadolescence, Adolescence, and College/Young Adulthood (described in Chapters 4 and 5). Biracial individuals continue to explore their biracial heritages as well as the heritages of others. "The integrated individual will find that he or she is able to function effectively in varying situations and understand different communities" (Kerwin & Ponterotto, 1995,

p. 214). Ongoing work is necessary in the lifelong process of integrating the various aspects that make up biracial identity.

The Continued Search for Appropriate Racial/Ethnic Identity Development Models for Interracial Adults

In addition to the empirical studies of adult biracial identity development just reviewed, there is a considerable body of literature related to racial/cultural/ethnic identity development models. The minority identity development (MID) model presented in Atkinson, Morten, and Sue's 1979 book, and revised in more recent editions (1983, 1989, 1993), has been introduced to many counselors. In 1990 Sue and Sue revised the MID and renamed it the Racial/ Cultural Identity Development (RCID) model.

The following are representative of culture-specific paradigms of racial/cultural/ethnic identity development. Parham and Helms (1981) researched the early Black identity development model of Cross (1971). A Black and White model of racial identity was proposed by Helms (1984, 1985, 1990). Kim (1981) presented a five-stage developmental model for Asian American racial identity development. Ruiz (1990) put forth a five-stage model of Chicano/Latino identity development. A model of White racial identity development was developed by Ponterotto (1988).

Racial/cultural/ethnic identity development models describe three to six stages that individuals experience in moving from a naiveté of their own racial identity to a sense of integration and fulfillment with their own racial identity (Wehrly, 1995). The stages between naiveté and integration may be marked with ambivalent and strong feelings about one's own racial group and about other racial groups. These models have been useful in assessment of the racial identity development of both the counselor and the counselee and provide clues for counselor interventions with clients at various levels of racial consciousness (Wehrly, 1995). *An unwritten assumption that seems to undergird most racial identity development models is that the individual has only one racial heritage with which to establish an identity.*

Limitations of Previous Models of Racial Identity Development for Biracial/Interracial Individuals

Recent authors have discussed the shortcomings of previous models of racial identity development when applied to biracial/interracial persons (Herring, 1995; Kerf-Wellington, 1992; Poston, 1990; Reynolds & Pope, 1991; Root, 1990). New models for the identity development of persons with more than one racial heritage have been presented (Kich, 1992; Poston, 1990; Reynolds & Pope, 1991; Root, 1990). Poston (1990) discussed four limitations of traditional racial identity models for application to biracial individuals. The following discussion of the limitations of traditional models of racial identity development is organized using Poston's framework.

1. At various stages in racial identity development, individuals are expected to choose one racial identity over another; this is not considered healthy for a person of biracial heritage. Participants in several of the empirical studies reviewed in this chapter reported pressures to choose one identity at some time in their lives (Brown, 1991, 1995; Hall, 1980, 1992; Kich, 1982, 1992; Murphy-Shigematsu, 1987; and Thornton, 1983). Interracial individuals writing in the popular press described pressures to "Choose One" (Courtney, 1995; Funderburg, 1994; Leslie et al., 1995; Steel, 1995; Williams, 1995).

2. The minority identity development models suggest that individuals first reject their minority culture and identity and then reject the dominant culture in order to attain a sense of fulfillment. Again, rejection of any racial identity is not seen as a healthy resolution of identity development for the interracial person. Interviewees in Funderburg's 1994 book, *Black, White, Other: Biracial Americans Talk About Race and Identity*, spoke to the issue of not wanting to reject one of their racial heritages. One person talked about wanting to value both parts of himself and not being able to hate half of himself.

Kich (1992) described the negative consequences for the Japanese Americans who chose the route of "taking sides" in their identity development. Root (1990) points out the difficulty of rejecting "Whiteness" if one is part White and suggests "that for those individuals who are part white to manifest hatred towards whiteness probably reflects oppression within the nuclear and extended family system" (p. 198). Root states that it is this aspect of the racial identity development models (usually the third stage) that is very inappropriate for the biracial or interracial person.

3. Racial identity models do not allow for the integration of multiple group identities. This factor seems especially important for interracial individuals who need to develop and integrate their racial identities from their multiple heritages (Anderson, 1993; Brown, 1995; Thornton, 1983).

4. Minority identity development models require acceptance into the minority culture of origin, especially during the immersion stage. Biracial individuals may not experience acceptance into either parent culture and may experience higher rates of victimization by parent and other cultures than minority persons do. The negative post–Civil War feelings of both Black and White people toward the thousands of mulattoes in their midst (described in Chapter 2) have lingered for more than a century in the minds of some people (Haizlip, 1994).

Root (1990) questions how the minority identity models can be applied to persons who are a minority-minority racial mix. If an interracial individual is of minority-minority racial mix and is not accepted by either of his or her parent cultures, the results can be devastating to the interracial person.

Poston's Biracial Identity Development Model

Poston's (1990) positive model of biracial identity development is designed to address the limitations of previous racial identity development models. He proposes five stages that the biracial individual experiences in attaining an integrated identity. The individual's reference group orientation attitudes change as the individual moves through these five stages.

In the first stage, *personal identity*, children's awareness of themselves is usually somewhat independent of their racial or ethnic backgrounds because of cognitive limitations. Reference group identity with racial or ethnic groups is not established; therefore, personal identity factors such as self-esteem that develop within their families are preeminent in their personal identity.

The second stage, *choice of group categorization*, occurs when biracial youth feel pressures to choose an ethnic or racial group identity. A variety of factors influence whether young people at this stage will select a multicultural categorization or a single racial identity. Some of the influencing factors are (a) status factors such as the group status of each parent's racial heritage, home neighborhood demographics, and peer group influence; (b) social support factors such as acceptance from each parent's family, participation in various cultural groups, and style and influence of the parents; and (c) personal factors such as physical appearance, knowledge of cultures and languages, and personality factors. Limited cognitive development for this age usually precludes choice of multiethnic identities.

In the third stage, *enmeshment/denial*, the biracial young person feels confusion and guilt over "having to choose one identity that is not fully expressive of one's background" (Poston, 1990, p. 154). Feelings of self-hatred and lack of acceptance by part of one's racial heritage are common. The biracial youth can "get stuck" at this level or broaden racial/ethnic perspectives to appreciate and own all of her or his heritage.

Appreciation, the fourth stage, is characterized by action to learn about and value all of one's racial heritages. Identification may still be with the group chosen at the second stage, but the individual is learning to accept and appreciate both or all aspects of her or his racial roots.

In the fifth stage, *integration*, biracial individuals have reached the point where they recognize and value all of their ethnic identities. "At this level, individuals develop a secure, integrated identity" (Poston, 1990, p. 154).

Poston recognizes that the most difficult periods for most biracial individuals are in the second and third stages when they feel forced to choose one racial reference group orientation. After becoming enmeshed with one reference group and denying part of their racial heritage, they may find it especially challenging to move out of these modes of adaptation.

Root's "Schematic Metamodel" for Resolution of Biracial Identity

A "schematic metamodel" with four possible resolutions of biracial identity is proposed by Root (1990). The model describes factors and criteria that determine each resolution and assumes that in each resolution biracial individuals recognize both sides of their racial heritages and are free to declare how they wish to identify themselves.

Root (1990) envisions her model as "a spiral where the linear force is internal conflict over a core sense of definition of self, the importance of which is largely determined by socialization (e.g., race, gender)" (p. 198). Conflict comes from different sources (such as conflict in the person's political, social, or familial environment). One or two significant conflicts occur during critical developmental periods in the lives of interracial people that may propel them to move forward. Root views the "tension between racial components within oneself . . . [as] the strongest recurring conflict at critical periods of development" (1990, p. 198). As a result of this omnipresent tension, the person experiences feelings of ambiguity, marginality, and discrimination.

The first resolution suggested by Root is for interracial individuals to *accept the identity that society assigns to them.* In parts of the United States where there is more racial oppression, the interracial individual may have stronger influences to accept a societally assigned identity. One of Funderburg's (1994) interviewees gave an example of this when she stated: "But I feel like when I walk down the streets or anything that I do in this world, people look at me as a black person or an African-American woman, and so I felt like I had to at some point accept that" (p. 204).

The first alternative is viewed as a passive resolution that is positive even though it may stem from oppressive influences on the interracial individual. This choice can be positive if the individual is happy with the choice assigned to her or him by external forces. The support and acceptance of the individual's extended family are important factors in making this a positive resolution and provide a secure reference group for the person.

Root sees the first resolution as the most tenuous of the four possible routes that the interracial individual may take because the individual could be viewed differently and assigned a different racial identity in a different part of the country. If interracial individuals choose to let society define their racial identity, they can show this as a positive choice through educating persons around them about their choice.

Identification with both (or all) racial groups is the second resolution discussed by Root (1990). She sees this resolution as positive if the personalities of the biracial/interracial individuals are similar in whatever racial group they operate and if they feel privileges from belonging to both (or all) groups. Some of the children interviewed in the Kerwin et al. (1993) research responded that they were "mixed." Half of the adolescents in the Gibbs and Hines (1992) study identified as "mixed." These young people would follow with explanations of their "mixed" heritage (e.g., "My Mom's Black and my Dad's White").

This resolution is seen as idealistic. Root (1990) notes that it may be available only in areas of the country where there are many people of more than one racial heritage (such as the West Coast). With recent publicity on interracial individuals and families in the popular press (e.g., Aubrey, 1995; Bates, 1993; Begley, 1995; Cose, 1995; Courtney, 1995; Funderburg, 1994; Haizlip, 1994, 1995; Leslie et al., 1995; Mathabane & Mathabane, 1992; Morganthau, 1995; Perkins, 1994; Pressley, 1994; Updike, 1992; von Sternberg, 1995a, 1995b; Williams, 1995), this resolution may soon be more acceptable in many parts of the United States.

Adopting the resolution does not change the way that society responds to interracial people, however. Interracial individuals who choose to identify with more than one racial group need to develop coping behaviors and claims to positive aspects of their heritages.

Root's third resolution is *identification with a single racial group*. This choice differs from the first alternative in that the individual chooses an identification regardless of whether this is the same identification that society might assign. If the choice selected by the individual is incongruent with the way that individual is viewed by others, there may be difficulties to face. Again, coping strategies are needed, and the individual may be called upon frequently to defend the choice. For some individuals, Root suggests that moving to another part of the country may make it easier to live with this resolution.

The fourth resolution offered by Root is *identification as a new racial group*. This is viewed as a positive resolution if it does not involve hiding or rejecting any part of one's racial heritage. The person may move freely among all racial groups, but consider himself or herself to be a part of a new group. Many of the individuals speaking in the popular press (cited previously) indicated the desire to identify not only with both or all of their racial heritage groups, but to also identify with a new biracial/interracial group. The search for others who were like self (biracial in heritage) was also described by several of Funderburg's interviewees. Root (1990) states that "A clear problem with this resolution is that society's classification system does not recognize persons of mixed race" (p. 201).

It is evident that Root emphasizes the need for interracial persons to develop coping strategies to deal with societal questions about their heritages so that these queries no longer leave people with the feeling that there is something wrong with them. (The cognitive behaviorists might call this stress inoculation.)

The four possible resolutions of interracial identity are not mutually exclusive. They may coexist and the individual may move among them. Root stresses the importance of interracial persons accepting both (or all) sides of their heritages as well as the importance of interracial persons having the freedom to choose their own identities.

Reynolds and Pope's Multidimensional Identity Model

After reviewing limitations of current identity development models, Reynolds and Pope (1991) outlined their Multidimensional Identity Model (MIM) (see Figure 6.1) built on Root's 1990 biracial identity development model. Their model addresses "the complexities of multiple identities and multiple oppressions" (Reynolds & Pope, 1991, p. 174). It challenges counselors to broaden and rethink alternatives for work with individuals experiencing multiple oppressions.

FIGURE 6.1 Multidimensional Identity Model

Identify with one aspect of self (society assigned—passive acceptance)	Identify with one aspect of self (conscious identification)
Identify with multiple aspects of self in a segmented fashion	Identify with combined aspects of self (identity intersection)

Note. From "The Complexities of Diversity: Exploring Multiple Oppressions" by A. L. Reynolds and R. L. Pope, 1991, *Journal of Counseling and Development, 70*, pp. 174–180. Copyright 1991 by *Journal of Counseling and Development*. Reprinted by permission.

Readers will note the similarity of the MIM to Root's "schematic metamodel" in the four possible resolutions of multiple identities and oppressions. In the Reynolds and Pope (MIM) adaptation of Root's model, individuals may choose to identify with part of their identity either passively or actively. Passive acceptance occurs when individuals let another person or group decide their identity for them. Active identification takes place when individuals consciously choose one part for self-identification. Either of these choices may involve actively suppressing one aspect of identification. A third option is to live in separate worlds in a segmented manner in order to identify with multiple aspects of self. The fourth option is to identify with a new group that combines all important identities.

Counselor Roles in Work with Interracial Adults

The preceding overview of biracial/interracial identity development paradigms implies several possible issues that the interracial adult may bring to counseling. However, Root (1994) calls attention to the fact that mixed-race women and men rarely come to counseling asking to resolve overt issues related to their interracial heritage. Counselor understanding of the possible impact of mixed racial heritage on the client is imperative for the therapist "to facilitate a relief of symptoms and/or strategize problem solving more quickly and in an appropriate context" (Root, 1994, p. 462).

Logan et al. (1987) also believe that underlying racial identity problems of biracial clients can have an impact on functioning in many areas of their lives. These authors note that biracial clients are referred for social work services for problems such as "inadequate social relationships, parent-child conflicts in their current families, and inadequate separation from their families of origin" (Logan et al., 1987, p. 14). In order to be effective in working with these problems, helping service workers usually have to also address racial identity issues.

Interracial adults have traveled paths to adulthood that have been heavily influenced by the significant others in their lives. The powerful impact of societal forces on the developing individual has been described in Chapters 4 and 5, which address counseling interracial children and adolescents. Root (1994) and Logan et al. (1987) present strategies for intervention with interracial adults that include consideration of the societal forces that have an impact on the individual.

A case example of a hypothetical biracial client, Carol, is presented first. Following this, concepts and interventions from the work of Root (1994), Logan et al. (1987), Spickard (1989), other authors, and my own clinical observations are discussed. Suggestions for applying some of these concepts to Carol's case are noted as appropriate.

CASE EXAMPLE

Carol is a 32-year-old White/Japanese female who has come for counseling because of issues related to lack of acceptance by co-workers, loneliness, and feeling that she does not belong. Carol has worked as a receptionist and bookkeeper at a local insurance office since she finished a two-year secretarial program at a local, rural, Midwest community college. She is the youngest of three children of a White U.S. serviceman who met and married her Japanese mother while he was with the Army of Occupation in Japan after World War II.

In 1952 Carol's mother came to the United States from Japan with her father and two older brothers. Her mother did everything she could to become "American" when she arrived in a rural Midwest community as the Japanese wife of a recently discharged White serviceman. She learned to communicate in English, cook "American" dishes, and sew "American" style clothing. She joined the local Lutheran Church of which her husband and family were members. Carol's mother did all of these things to try to please her husband and his parents.

Carol's two brothers are in their mid-40s and have lived on the West Coast since they finished their graduate degrees in chemistry and mathematics. Both brothers married White "American" women and have maintained minimal contact with their parents and Carol since they married. Because Carol's brothers were in high school when she was born, she never felt close to them.

Carol's paternal grandparents have always praised her for being such a good "American" granddaughter. They take great pride that she looks more like her blonde Scandinavian father than her dark-haired Japanese mother. Since she was a little girl, Carol's paternal grandparents have praised her for keeping her hair short and "permed."

Carol says that she never felt close to either set of her grandparents. Before their deaths in the 1980s, her Japanese grandparents occasionally wrote to her mother. Because the letters were written in Japanese, Carol had to depend on her mother to translate them. To Carol, the letters seemed overly formal and lacking in real news.

Carol remembers that in high school she was encouraged to run for prom queen because she was told she had that "exotic" look. She also remembers being teased behind her back for her "Chinka, chinka Chinaman" eyes.

As an outstanding student in both high school and community college, Carol's classmates came to her for help on their homework. Often, they talked Carol into letting them copy her homework. Carol noticed, however, that the same students did not ask her to join their social cliques. Being the only biracial student in her school led to feeling that she did not belong in any group. Her energies were spent toward serving as editor of the high school newspaper and the high school yearbook.

For years Carol has attended and worked in the church of her father's family. Recently she realized that she receives little satisfaction through her church-related activities.

Carol is also dissatisfied with the relationships that she has had with men. She notices that men seem to be attracted to her "exotic" appearance, but do not want to enter into deep and long-lasting relationships. She feels that she has been exploited sexually. Lately, she has turned down all opportunities for male companionship.

At work, Carol has suffered verbal sexual harassment from her boss, but she feels that she cannot complain because he pays her well and gives her generous fringe benefits. Her coworkers are polite and friendly on a superficial basis, but she never seems able to develop real friendships with them.

Carol asks the counselor what to do about living life as an outsider most of the time. She says that at times she is very lonely and depressed and stays in her apartment reading or watching television when she has free time.

Root's Themes for Counseling Interracial People

Six general themes related to being interracial are discussed by Root (1994): *uniqueness, acceptance and belonging, physical appearance, sexuality, self-esteem,* and *identity.*

Uniqueness. The quality of being different and unique is a very important aspect of any interracial individual's life. Root (1994) notes that this theme interfaces with all of the other themes of interracial existence. Dealing with this theme of uniqueness could be assessed as pathological if not understood by counselors.

The uniqueness quality is especially significant for multiracial adult women who may alternately feel special and hurt and angry. If life situations occur to disrupt this feeling of being special or unique, the individual may feel angry, alienated, or depressed. Feelings may appear to be more intense than the issues discussed seem to warrant. Root outlines the therapist's role as helping the interracial woman "to understand if and how these feelings are related to the multiracial experience, how to interpret the feeling, and how to cope" (Root, 1994, p. 463). Because men have been conditioned to restrain their feelings more than women, similar feelings may or may not surface in counseling interracial men.

The therapist may notice that some multiracial adults personalize events that seem to perpetuate feeling misunderstood and different since they have always lived as unique individuals. Root states that this lifestyle can lead to a style of communicating that provides much context in order to help others understand one's uniqueness, a style of communicating that may look compulsive and even paranoid to others. The counselor has noted that Carol gives very detailed and contextualized accounts when she discusses her problems.

Living as a unique individual all of one's life sometimes leads to strong feelings of isolation and depression. This may be particularly applicable to women because they, more than men, validate themselves through sharing with significant people. Carol seems to give evidence of this. Her ongoing feelings of depression will need to be addressed by the counselor.

Both men and women interviewed by Funderburg (1994) spoke of the desire for opportunities to share with other interracial adults. Counselors can play an important role in helping their clients locate such a support group. If there is no interracial support group in the area, counselors can be instrumental in helping to organize one. In Carol's case, the counselor may or may not find a support group anywhere in the area nor enough biracial people to start one. If Carol can get to Chicago, she might enjoy participating in one of the interracial support groups operating in that area.

Because the multiple heritages of interracial people have given them unique perspectives on society, they may seem to put more faith in their own perspectives than in the perceptions of others. As a defense mechanism related to their own insecurity, some interracial youth (particularly young women) take on the role of being the chief negotiator between their family, their peers, and the larger society. After Carol's older brothers left home, she took on the negotiator role in her family. Root notes that this perspective might be interpreted as indicative of a dysfunctional family when, in reality, it is the larger society in which the multiracial individual lives that is dysfunctional. An area for the counselor to explore in Carol's case is whether Carol wants to continue the negotiator role for her family, and, if not, if she is willing to relinquish this role.

Acceptance and Belonging. Interracial individuals' challenges to feeling accepted start as soon as they are old enough to interact with their worlds and have been described throughout this book. A lifetime of hearing insensitive questions and teasing does not provide a positive base for feeling connected to others. Feelings of rejection, anger, and hurt need to be validated by the counselor.

Difficulties in belonging are intensified during adolescence when peer group acceptance and inclusion is paramount. These difficulties in belonging may continue into adulthood for interracial individuals such as Carol. Criteria for acceptance into groups vary; however, persons with more than one racial heritage may find it difficult to gain full acceptance into our contemporary multiracial society because they do not meet rigid criteria established by various groups. Physical appearance can rule them out because they do not "look like" others of the group to which they wish to belong. Carol has already shared how difficult it was as a teenager to hear others making fun of her appearance behind her back.

Biracial individuals may be accepted into a racial group to increase the numbers, thus giving the group more political power. Acceptance into a group on this basis does not necessarily mean that friendship will be extended to the biracial individual. Sometimes this leads to the multiracial person's taking on negative stereotypical behaviors of a particular group in an attempt to be accepted.

Counselor acknowledgment of the very real social environmental barriers that the mixed race client faces is important. These barriers can lead to increased feelings of loneliness and isolation and leave clients vulnerable to anxiety and depression. The counselor can help the client examine the productiveness of the strategies she or he is employing in order to fit in or belong.

In Carol's case, the counselor needs to let Carol know that she recognizes the social and environmental barriers that Carol faces. The counselor might explore if Carol felt exploited by her peers when they copied her homework or by her boss when he engages in verbal sexual harassment. Is Carol allowing these things to happen in attempts to get accepted? If Carol recognizes this as exploitation, what steps is she ready to take to change this behavior? If assertive behavior could help, Carol may need some role-playing practice during counseling sessions to get the courage to make major behavior changes in the way she reacts verbally to others.

It is also important to explore whether the client is rejecting or denouncing part of her or his heritage in this attempt to belong. This area might best be explored with Carol in conjunction with the genogram, ecomap, and the Cultural Continuum to be described in the discussion of suggestions from Logan et al. (1987).

Interracial clients may also need to know that feeling different is OK and that on different days and in different situations they may feel differently. This could be an area to explore with Carol. The counselor can also help Carol brainstorm about advantages that she feels from being part of more than one group.

Physical Appearance. Root notes three types of unique experiences related to physical appearance that the mixed-race person may encounter. One is having a name that does not fit with one's appearance. This situation can lead to questions as to whether this is a married name or whether one is adopted. The counselor could ask Carol if having a name that does not fit her "exotic" appearance has ever bothered her.

The endless stares that the interracial individual encounters are the second type of experience and can lead to feelings of ongoing evaluation by others. Carol has not reported this, but it may be an area that needs exploration. Root cautions against the therapist's assuming that these feelings are irrational because there may be a strong reality base present for this interpretation. Cognitive therapy to dispel irrational beliefs may be inappropriate.

The third experience suggested by Root relates to the flexibility of appearance of which the interracial individual is capable. This heightens the need for the person to establish a consistent internal identity that does not need to be validated by the environment. Root notes that the behavior of "playing with" one's flexible look beyond adolescence "does not necessarily indicate pathology or lack of a stable identity, but may instead reflect valuing of different pieces of the person's identity . . . or even a conscious or unconscious challenge to society's social order" (Root, 1994, p. 468). This behavior is more common in women and teenage girls than in men and boys. In Carol's case, the counselor may need more information before deciding how much Carol needs validation from her environment in order to feel good about her physical appearance. Also, how do situational contexts influence the way Carol's physical appearance is perceived and how does she respond? The counselor might encourage Carol to "play with" racial and ethnic appearance at times to see how others will respond.

Another issue related to unique physical appearance is that other people may make assumptions about an individual's racial identity based on physical appearance and subsequent interactions with the mixed-race individual may be based on these assumptions (Logan et al., 1987). Wijeyesinghe (1992) found that physical appearance was one of three factors having the most influence on choice of racial identity.

The aspect of physical appearance may be an especially vulnerable issue for interracial women because of the value that society places on appearance as an asset for women. Root notes that physical appearance can also be a double-edged sword for the multiracial woman. Exotic looking models may be highly valued, but in daily life the ongoing questions and stares can turn one's physical appearance into a burden. Carol has already given the counselor information that illustrates this when she told about being encouraged to run for high school prom queen but being teased behind her back about her different eyes.

Counselors' work with interracial clients' issues of physical appearance can easily reflect the counselors' biases related to this issue. Distinguishing normative behavior from dysfunctional behavior is imperative in helping to empower clients.

Sexuality. The area of sexuality is an appropriate one for counselors to explore with interracial clients, but sexuality as an issue for interracial men has rarely been addressed in the counseling literature. Multiracial women report oppression and discrimination in the area of sexuality more than multiracial men. The old myths of the exotic sexual attractiveness of the multiracial female persist. For some women the myth provides permission to be sexual; for others the myths seem to lead to curtailing sexuality. Root also believes that some mixed-race women are more open to exploring sexual orientation because they have a lifetime of living with flexibility. Carol's lack of satisfaction with previous sexual relationships will probably make this a very significant area of counselor and client work.

Some mixed-race women enter into sexual relationships that seem to be based on fantasies loaded with racial or gender stereotypes. These relationships may be the result of a hunger for acceptance or basing one's specialness on one's appearance. In the end these women usually feel emotionally unfulfilled. Root encourages counselors to explore whether a history of sexual or emotional abuse may leave mixed-race women vulnerable to experiences of being treated like objects to possess.

Carol recognizes that her sexual relationships were affected by both racial and gender stereotypes and a desire to feel accepted. She admits both sexual and emotional abuse by some of the males with which she had relationships. Her boss's harassment has been limited to inappropriate verbalizations and innuendoes. Counselor and client work in the area of sexuality is needed and will probably overlap with work in the areas of acceptance, belonging, and physical appearance.

Self-Esteem. For some interracial people the concept of being different or special equates with the necessity to be outstanding or extra good in order to feel good about themselves. When mixed-race individuals base their worth on this necessity to excel, they may develop fragile feelings of self-worth and fluid concepts of self. The person with a fluid concept of self will be very controlled by external events. As I have noted elsewhere, when an individual has a fluid concept of self, "the self is as the self does" (Wehrly, 1995, p. 16).

The historic perceptions of interracial individuals as having a higher incidence of problems and poor self-esteem seem to have become self-fulfilling prophecies for some people with more than one heritage. However, recent studies of nonclinical biracial adolescents and adults (Alipuria, 1990; Gibbs & Hines, 1992; Hall, 1980, 1992; Kerwin, 1991) have not supported the negative self-esteem perceptions of earlier writers.

An area for the counselor to explore with Carol is how much her feelings of self-worth are based on external evaluations. Root cautions that counselors who are not aware of their own internalized oppressive beliefs about multiracial people may inaccurately conclude that low self-esteem is the basis of the problems of multiracial clients.

Identity. Identity issues of interracial individuals have been addressed throughout this book. Having a sense of identity equates with having a sense of belonging.

The models of interracial identity development delineated earlier in this chapter provide the counselor with a framework for assessing levels of development and choices of identity made by the interracial client. Selection of an appropriate model (or models) to use in client assessment and treatment will depend on counselor-client interactions and on the client's style of learning.

The three stages outlined in Kich's model can help the counselor and Carol examine behaviors that indicate the stages of multiracial or interracial development that she has experienced since childhood. Poston's five stages of attaining an integrated biracial identity might be another paradigm for looking at Carol's racial identity development. Root's 1990 metamodel for four possible resolutions of biracial identity and Reynolds and Pope's 1991 Multidimensional Identity Model provide other perspectives for examining Carol's racial identity. In how many of Root's four possible resolutions for her biracial identity has Carol operated in the past and present? How does she describe her comfort level in the various resolutions?

Additional clues to Carol's racial self-identification will come when the counselor and client work together to examine the Logan et al. (1987) Cultural Continuum to be explained in the next section.

Logan, Freeman, and McRoy's
Ecological Practice Approach

This approach is composed of assessment and interventions and is discussed separately under these categories. In actual practice, the interventions overlap and are interrelated rather than being a neat two-phase process. The ultimate goal of this ecological approach is to help clients become bicultural.

Several possible components of *assessment* are suggested. One is direct observation of the client by the counselor. Listen for the way that Carol refers to her racial identity and whether others are blamed for racial identity issues. Watch for nonverbal behavior that indicates uneasiness and discomfort when racial identity issues are discussed.

Three other process-oriented procedures are recommended for assessment in work with biracial clients. The first is the use of the *genogram*. Work on the genogram can begin as soon as a positive working relationship is established with Carol. Construction of the genogram will help the counselor and Carol examine racial identity issues in the context of the family. Logan et al. (1987) suggest that in addition to the usual areas explored with the genogram (relationships within the family, patterns of communication, emotional cut-offs, family events that have been significant, assignment of roles, etc.), additional questions need to be explored with interracial clients.

Areas unique to Carol's interracial family to explore are racial heritages of parents and siblings; attitudes of family members toward the differing racial heritages of family members; how the family and others assign racial labels to Carol; how Carol labels herself racially; patterns and themes in both functional and dysfunctional areas across generations (this might be impossible to assess for the relatives still living in Japan); moves that the family has made related to their mixed-race heritage; and "lifestyle factors related to racial backgrounds such as childbearing practices, health patterns, dietary habits, causes of stress and patterns of coping with it, occupational choices, marital relationships, and economic conditions" (Logan et al., 1987, p. 15). Gathering this information can also help the counselor and Carol summarize both strengths and problems and provide a basis for discussion of changes that she desires.

The second process-oriented technique recommended by Logan et al. (1987) is construction of an *ecomap*. This can be adapted to reflect issues unique to being of mixed race. The same kinds of connecting lines and symbols to indicate relationships are used in the ecomap as in a genogram. In a sense, the ecomap (see Figure 6.2) is an extension of the genogram. Members of the client's family or household are listed in a large central circle. Connections between the family and other social systems are represented by circles around the central family household circle using connecting lines like those used in a genogram to represent relationships.

Construction of the ecomap with Carol can follow discussion of her genogram. The ecomap provides the opportunity to observe what external social systems (such as work, education, extended family, peer, and leisure time) are seen as placing pressure on Carol. Carol's ecomap will probably indicate current stressful situations at work and a past stressful situation with a live-in boyfriend. Relations with her paternal grandparents indicate a tenuous situation in spite of much energy flowing in both directions. Her past involvement with her church has meant a heavy outflow of energy but a tenuous situation as far as satisfaction derived for Carol. The counselor and Carol should work to find a balance between supportive and conflictual environmental relationships.

Logan et al. (1987) recommend exploring additional questions with interracial clients as the client and counselor work to develop the ecomap:

1. What role models for positive racial identity development are present? In Carol's case, her brothers may be the only role models she can name.
2. What cut-offs related to racial identity issues are there? Carol is totally cut off from her maternal relatives and somewhat cut off from her brothers.

FIGURE 6.2 Ecomap for Carol

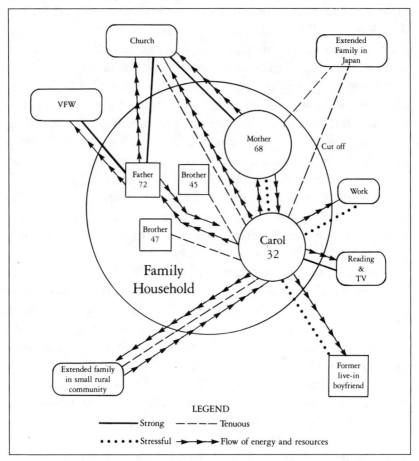

Note. Revised and reprinted with permission from the *Journal of Intergroup Relations* (the official quarterly of the National Association of Human Rights Workers), 1987, Volume 15, No. 1, p. 20.

3. When and how did these cut-offs occur and how have these cut-offs affected the client's functioning? The cut-off with Carol's maternal grandparents occurred before she was born and was finalized when they died. The partial cut-offs with her brothers occurred when she was a young girl. This has left her feeling isolated from her brothers.

4. Can Carol's negative perspectives of her situation be reframed to reflect positive strengths? If Carol becomes interested in studying her Japanese heritage, she may find many positive

Japanese values that are reflected in her daily life. She might also find it advantageous to play with her identity in various situations and see what results this brings.

5. Are there sources of support for Carol that she has ignored? Carol's brothers and their families might provide support if she can learn how to reach out to them.

The third process-oriented intervention strategy recommended by Logan et al. (1987) is the *cultural continuum* (see Figure 6.3). "The cultural continuum is a tool for helping mixed-race clients identify how they have adapted to their racial backgrounds and the potential consequences for that stance and other options" (Logan et al., 1987, p. 16).

The cultural continuum shows the extent of individual adaptation to one's racial background. On the cultural continuum this adapta-

FIGURE 6.3 The Cultural Continuum

Denial of the importance of race and culture (color-blind perception).	*Complete assimilation within the dominant culture.*	*Complete assimilation within the relevant minority culture.*	*Bicultural or multicultural.*
ADVANTAGES			
Avoidance of pain associated with working through racial identity issues.	Greater acceptance by and blending in with dominant culture when successfully assimilated.	Greater group support, maintenance of the minority culture, and possibility of positive racial identity.	Increased ability to function effectively in two or more cultures, access to resources in the dominant culture as well as those of minority culture, and cultural maintenance.
DISADVANTAGES			
Lack of connection with and support from any culture, denial of self, and failure to handle conflictual views of society about racial identity.	Loss of culture, traditions, and group support from the rejected cultural group.	Limited access to resources available in dominant culture and loss of opportunities to learn about the positive effects of cultural diversity.	Risk of failing in two or more cultures, and emotional stress associated with adapting to more than one culture.

Note. Reprinted with permission from the *Journal of Intergroup Relations* (the official quarterly of the National Association of Human Rights Workers), 1987, Volume 15, No. 1, p. 17.

tion to racial background ranges from denying the importance of culture (saying that one is neutral and that culture is not important) to biculturalism (open expressions of interest in both, or all, of one's cultural heritage). The cultural continuum notes advantages and disadvantages for four different cultural identifications along the continuum.

Carol can study the continuum with the counselor, decide where she "is" on the scale, and discuss issues such as the following with the counselor.

1. What behavioral evidence supports Carol's selection of a particular spot on the continuum?
2. How aware is Carol of the various options for identification with her cultural heritages and of the advantages and disadvantages of these levels of cultural identifications?
3. Is Carol satisfied with her current choice of cultural identification? If not, what does she want to do about making changes in identification with her cultures of origin?
4. Are there individuals on Carol's genogram or ecomap that represent the cultural continuum point where she would like to be? How might Carol use the identified individual (or individuals) to aid in moving to a different spot on the cultural continuum?

Use of these three process-oriented tools during the counseling sessions (the genogram, the ecomap, and the cultural continuum) is a nonpathological procedure to help interracial clients clarify "if and to what extent racial identity issues are problematic for them" (Logan et al., 1987, p. 16). The procedures also help in identifying positive supports for Carol's racial identity.

Other Counseling Techniques

Because Carol is an avid reader, she might enjoy searching the literature to study both sides of her racial heritage, the Swedish American and the Japanese, as out-of-session assignments. There are now a host of sources for studying culture and history. One of the traditional sources is the *Harvard Encyclopedia of American Ethnic Groups* edited by Thernstrom (1980). Two of the nine volumes of the more recent *Encyclopedia of World Cultures* could provide more comprehensive information on Carol's Swedish and Japanese backgrounds: Volume 4, *Europe*, edited by Bennett (1992) and Volume 5, *East and Southeast Asia*, edited by Hockings (1993). Parts I and II, "Japanese Americans" and "Madam Butterfly Revisited," of Spickard's 1989 book, *Mixed Blood*, contain information on the history and background of the Japanese in America. Part II, "Madam Butterfly Revisited," might be of special interest to Carol because it delineates the sociopolitical situation in Japan when her father served with the U.S. Army of Occupation and met and married her mother. Part II also discusses the sociopolitical situation in the United States at the time that her parents came to settle here. Content of Part II of Spickard could provide material for discussions with her parents.

Novels are an especially pleasant way for some people to learn about culture and history. In the past three decades many ethnic novels and autobiographies have made the best-seller lists (e.g., *I Know Why the Caged Bird Sings* [Angelou, 1970]; *The Joy Luck Club* [Tan, 1989]; *Bless Me Ultima* [Anaya, 1973]; and *Soul Catcher* [Herbert, 1984]). Novels and stories about biracial/interracial people are of more recent origin (e.g., *Black, White, Other: Biracial Americans Talk About Race and Ethnicity* [Funderburg, 1994], *Life on the Color Life* [Williams, 1995]; and *The Sweeter the Juice* [Haizlip, 1994]). Carol might find it interesting to read how these people have, and are, negotiating life in the United States. Content of any of this kind of out-of-session reading could make for interesting discussions with the counselor.

Summary

The chapter has addressed several topics related to counseling interracial adults. After an introduction and a section reiterating the importance of counselor self-awareness related to work with interracial people, issues faced by interracial adults were discussed. Several empirical research studies of biracial people were reviewed. A brief overview of traditional models of racial/ethnic identity development and a discussion of the limitations of these models for people with more than one racial heritage followed. Models of biracial/interracial identity development and resolution were presented.

The chapter closed with a discussion of counselor roles with interracial adults through integrating theory and practice with Carol, a hypothetical biracial White/Japanese adult. The overview of counselor interventions with Carol provided a far from exhaustive sample of many possibilities for helping service work with an interracial adult client. It is recognized, however, that in actual practice, the counselor would not employ all of these strategies.

7

Counseling
Interracial Families

F amilies become interracial in a variety of ways:
through cross-racial marriage, cross-racial co-
habitation, cross-racial adoption, cross-racial foster
home care, and cross-racial single parenting. This chapter introduces readers to interracial family counseling
issues and discusses counseling interventions appropriate for this population. Given the breadth of the topic,
the chapter will be limited to an overview, rather than
in-depth treatment, of topics related to interracial family counseling.

The chapter is organized under these headings: .
Counselor Self-Awareness as the First Step in Counseling Interracial Families, Issues Faced by Interracial

Families, Counselor Roles in Work with Interracial Families, Psychoeducational Counselor Roles With Interracial Families, Other Counselor Roles With Interracial Families, and Special Considerations for Counseling with Families That Have Become Interracial Through Cross-Racial Adoption or Cross-Racial Foster Home Placement.

Counselor Self-Awareness as the First Step in Counseling Interracial Families

The necessity for counselors to be aware of their own internalized prejudices and racism is emphasized by several of the writers addressing helping service work with interracial families (Adler, 1987; Baptiste, 1990; Brown, 1987; Davidson, 1992; Faulkner & Kich, 1983; Gibbs, 1989; Sebring, 1985; Shackford, 1984). These authors encourage counselors to examine their own beliefs, values, and stereotypes related to race, ethnicity, and interracial marriage. Brown (1987) discusses how the individual racism of the helper can impede the therapeutic process. Faulkner and Kich (1983) state that "The family therapist working with an interracial couple and their children must be sensitive and self-aware, especially in the beginning phases of treatment while gathering information about the family's life cycle as well as when incorporating the racial and ethnic dimensions within their problem-definition" (p. 80).

Counselors are alerted to review the process of self-examination of attitudes, beliefs, and values outlined in Chapter 3 under the section Counselor Self-Study of Ethnic/Racial Heritage as a first step in work with interracial families.

Issues Faced by Interracial Families

Although legal barriers to cross-racial marriage were struck down with the 1967 Loving v. Virginia U.S. Supreme Court decision, social sanctions to interracial marriage are still present with many people and in many parts of the United States. In 1984 Shackford discussed how all interracial children had to cope with the problems of racism that other children of color had to deal with and "with outsiders who view their normal, loving, strong families as pathological, unstable and peculiar" (p. 5). Eight years later Davidson (1992) stated that

> even when the interracial family system itself is functional, the continued negative attitudes held about interracial couples and their children and the prejudiced behavior the couples may face in the workplace, in housing, with friends, and with the family . . . set the stage for difficulties in personal and social adjustment. (p. 151)

Davidson anticipated that the resurgence of racism in the United States would lead to an increased need for therapists to be ready to work with interracial couples and their families.

Myths still abound about the reasons that individuals choose to marry someone of another race. As discussed in Chapter 1, some people remain convinced that one or both partners of an interracial couple are rebelling against their parents. Other myths are that anyone who chooses to marry cross-racially has ulterior motives or deep-seated psychological problems. Davidson (1992) lists several other theories about interracial coupling (e.g., sexual curiosity, economic advantages, and exhibitionism). Myths such as these are difficult to dispel and may cloud the issues brought to counseling by interracial families.

Societal reservations seem to be particularly strong against African American interracial marriage. Sebring (1985) noted that problems are especially evident for the "first-generation" children of one Black and one White parent because of "culturally imposed differences between races and the ways in which having parents of both races confounds the process of forming an ethnic identity" (p. 5). Many of these objections to Black/White intermarriage were generated by White people during the period of slavery, strengthened in the Jim Crow era, and perpetuated throughout much of the 20th century (Spickard, 1989).

Not all objections to Black outmarriage come from White people, however. Graham devoted an entire chapter to the reasons why some Black people oppose interracial marriage in his 1995 book, *Member of the Club.* This author recognized that outsiders may consider Black opposition to intermarriage as Black bigotry and discussed the following six objections that some Black people have to interracial coupling:

> **Objection 1**: When a black leader or advocate marries outside the race, his decision may be evidence that he will demonstrate less commitment to black people and our causes. (p. 36)
> **Objection 2**: We fear that intermarrying blacks are making a statement to black and white America that black spouses are less desirable partners—and are, therefore, inferior. (p. 40)
> **Objection 3**: Interracial marriage undermines our ability to introduce our black children to black mentors and role models who accept their racial identity with confidence and pride. (p. 45)
> **Objection 4**: Because it diffuses our resources, interracial marriage makes it difficult to build a black America that has uncompromised wealth, prestige, and power, thus making it harder to empower other parts of black America and erase the stereotypes of a weak and impoverished black community. (p. 49)
> **Objection 5**: We worry that confused biracial children will turn their backs on the black race once they discover it's easier to live as a white person. (p. 50)
> **Objection 6**: Today's interracial relationships are a painful reminder of a 250-year period in black American history when our sexuality was exploited beyond our control and to our detriment by white people. (p. 54)

Interracial couples may come to counseling and want to discuss the objections to Black interracial marriage presented by Graham.

Three major themes and several minor themes emerged from Kerwin's interviews with parents in her study of the biracial identity development of offspring of Black/White racial heritages (Kerwin, 1991). The first major theme was that of the "use or nonuse of racially identifying labels for the family and the child or children" (Kerwin et al., 1993, p. 225). Preparing the children for anticipated discrimination was the second major theme that emerged in Kerwin's study. The issue of choosing where the family would live to bring up their biracial child or children was the third major theme. Minor themes from the parent interviews were (a) patterns of friendship for the family as a unit and for individual members of the family, (b) extended family relationships, (c) religious affiliations, and (d) schools. Any or all of these themes may be brought as issues for interracial family counseling.

Mura (1992) described challenges he was facing in teaching his biracial Japanese American/White daughter about her dual racial heritage and how to deal with racism. These two challenges are similar to the first two themes that Kerwin reported in her interviews with Black/White interracial families.

Some parents may need help to feel comfortable with their own racial heritages and with the impact of these heritages on the family constellation. Communication among members of the interracial family often needs improvement. Interracial adolescents, in particular, have reported a desire to have more family discussions on racism and ethnic identity issues (Gibbs & Hines, 1992).

In Kerwin's research, the interracial families that frequently involved their children and adolescents in family discussions of racial issues, and that encouraged open dialogue with others, were the families in which the offspring "were found to be more likely to describe themselves with an interracial label and to perceive themselves as having membership in both groups" (Kerwin et al., 1993, p. 230). The young people in these families also seemed to discuss racial issues more openly with the interviewer and to be aware of both advantages and disadvantages of their biracial heritage.

Parents of biracial children and adolescents may need help in understanding the process their children experience in attempting to establish a racial identity (Gibbs & Hines, 1992; Jacobs, 1977, 1992). This racial identity development process often includes a period of turbulence in family relationships, including periods of rejection of one or both of the parents by their interracial children as well as adolescent peer pressures to choose one racial identity. Poston (1990) underscores the importance of parental and community support in helping biracial adolescents through the stages of racial identity development.

A specific issue that interracial families may bring to the counselor is how to handle questions about the physical appearance of their children who look like neither parent and who are judged by White standards of beauty. This issue may arise in any family with more than one racial heritage. As noted in previous chapters, the physical appearance of an individual has major implications for the way society will perceive and treat a person of mixed heritage.

In writing about important issues in family counseling with gifted and talented Black students, Exum (1983) recognized that some of the students about whom he was writing were members of a biracial family in which one or both parents might be Anglo-American. This author underscored the social significance of looking non-White and emphasized that families need to confront issues of racial ambiguity faced by biracial Black gifted students because "The students who appear to be Black will eventually be treated as if they are Black; if not in their own communities, then certainly elsewhere in this country" (Exum, 1983, p. 31). Contemporary reports indicate that Exum's statement is still accurate more than a decade later (Cose, 1995; Courtney, 1995; Funderburg, 1994; Haizlip, 1994, 1995; Leslie et al., 1995; Morganthau, 1995; Rosenblatt, Karis, & Powell, 1995; Steel, 1995).

Readers have probably noted that the literature on Black-White interracial families is more abundant than literature on other interracial families. A few authors have addressed issues of other interracial couples and families.

Mar's 1988 doctoral dissertation investigated the interracial parenting and ethnic identity challenges of Chinese/Caucasian families. Mar found that these interracial couples did not see the ethnic identity of their biracial children as an issue. The ethnic identity of the Caucasian parent received far less attention than the ethnic identity of the Chinese parent. Considerable concern about the children losing their Chinese culture was evident. Mar also noted that cultural conflicts in these families often revolved around family role expectations. This could be an area for counselors to explore in counseling with interracial Chinese/Caucasian families.

Rose (1984) discussed the complexities of biracial, bicultural Hispanic families. These complexities are compounded when Hispanic couples come from different Spanish-speaking countries, "each with its own cultural heritage, racial composition, patterns of immigration and emigration" (Rose, 1984, p. 12). Intermarriage for Hispanics in the United States may result in different combinations of cultures (e.g., first-generation Spanish-dominant Hispanics and second- or third-generation English-dominant Hispanics as well as Hispanics who have intermarried with people of other races). Attitudes toward intermarriage among Hispanics vary and can be a source of friction within the interracial Hispanic family. Rose also emphasized that majority culture negative attitudes toward the Spanish language reinforce messages that the Anglo culture is superior.

Baptiste (1990) reviewed issues brought to therapy by two kinds of Black/Hispanic families: Black/Hispanic immigrants and Black/Hispanic Americans. Most Black/Hispanic immigrants speak Spanish, whereas most Black/Hispanic Americans do not speak Spanish. Although Black/Hispanics are members of both the Hispanic and Black minority groups, their acceptance is marginal by both groups. "They, however, share equally the societally-imposed minority status and experience the societal prejudice directed at both" (Baptiste, 1990, p. 16). A variety of issues may be brought by either type of Black/Hispanic family, such as identity confusion, depreciated self-image, social marginality, ostracism, isolation, and sibling problems due to different skin colors.

Johnson and Nagoshi (1986) compared the adjustment of offspring of within-group and interracial/intercultural marriages in Hawaii. Their results suggested "that children of cross-ethnic marriages are not much different from children of within-ethnic marriages in Hawaii, and what few significant differences are present do not produce a pattern suggesting any kind of increased risk of adjustment problems for the former group" (Johnson & Nagoshi, 1986, p. 282). The authors noted that there is very little societal stigma associated with cross-ethnic marriages in Hawaii and speculated that "a good case might be made that such stigma and the stresses it imposes on the family are the key variables producing whatever generalized negative effect of such marriages on offspring as might be found elsewhere" (Johnson & Nagoshi, 1986, p. 283).

Cottrell (1990) presents an insightful perspective in her summary of a review of the literature on cross-national marriage when she notes "Cultural differences do not necessarily mean interpersonal conflict. . . . in the long run it is not the cultural difference per se, but rather personal rigidity regarding these differences which account for interpersonal conflict" (p. 165). A major issue for the counselor to "sort out" is how much of the rigidity springs from the individual personalities of family members, how much rigidity arises from and maintains systemic patterns in the family as a whole, and how much rigidity is a response to the outer society that interacts with the interracial family.

Counselor Roles in Work With Interracial Families

Faulkner and Kich (1983) state that "Without an awareness of or sensitivity to the complex dynamics of the multiracial family system, therapists may inadvertently drive away their clients after the initial sessions" (p. 79). Counseling with an interracial family can take on many dimensions that are not present in counseling with a mono-racial family. When a counselor meets with an interracial family, the counselor is dealing with people of at least three racial/ethnic groups. Parents will bring differing worldviews and differing assumptions regarding behavior. The children will bring additional worldviews. Counseling interventions need to be tailored to meet the unique dynamics and needs of each family. Steps in assessment and engagement of family members to determine the stress that has brought the family for help, as well as treatment decisions, may be compounded by the interracial composition of the family.

CASE EXAMPLE

In Chapter 5, Rose, a 10th-grade interracial adolescent with an African American father and a Mexican American/Navajo mother, was referred to the high school counselor, Mr. Wood, for fighting at school and for low achievement. Mr. Wood's counseling interventions with Rose and with other school personnel were described in Chapter 5.

After several sessions with Mr. Wood, Rose suggested that it would really help for the family to have counseling. Mr. Wood and Rose then met with Rose's parents, Mr. and Mrs. Morris.

The family agreed to go to a local mental health center for family counseling in order to help Rose. The Morris family called for an appointment at a local mental health center, went for an intake, and were assigned to Raymond Gonzales, a Mexican American counselor. Rose has given Mr. Gonzales permission to talk with her high school counselor, Mr. Wood.

The next sections discuss roles in which the counselor may be involved with the interracial family, including several specific techniques for implementing these roles. Some of the therapeutic interventions discussed will be related specifically to work with the Morris interracial family.

Assessment and Engagement of the Interracial Family

The processes of assessing and engaging the interracial family occur simultaneously. The guidelines for developing a cross-cultural relationship described in Chapter 3 are pertinent to assessment and engagement of the interracial family. Areas of focus for assessment and techniques for engagement are described separately here even though these processes and techniques will be used concurrently by the counselor.

Assessment of the Interracial Family. Faulkner and Kich (1983) recommend examining at least three areas to determine the strengths and weaknesses of the interracial family: (a) *family life cycle*, (b) *intimacy and boundaries*, and (c) *interracial children's responses*. The areas are not mutually exclusive, so exploration of one area may also give information on one or both of the other areas.

The developmental phase of a *family's life cycle* can have a major impact on issues brought by the interracial family. The differing racial/cultural backgrounds of the couple have significant influences on the way(s) in which these developmental phases are negotiated in each interracial family. Faulkner and Kich (1983) see the important family life cycles as:

the beginning family (courtship, engagement, marriage); birth of first child; the sharing of influence with other authorities when the child enters school; the family with adolescents; the family as a launching center (the offsprings' separation from home and marriage); the family in its middle years; and the aging family (with return to single life at the death of a spouse). (p. 81)

As the family moves through the phases of their life cycle they will be influenced by the responses from their families of origin. The support of the extended families on either (or both) sides may be missing as the family experiences these phases. Sometimes grandparents, uncles, aunts, and cousins do not accept the children as relatives (Gibbs, 1987). Sometimes members of the extended family treat interracial children in a demeaning way or make racist remarks about the children's parents. Negative treatment by the extended family may result in feelings of hurt, anger, and disappointment. Additionally, such negative treatment is likely to create and maintain dysfunctional patterns of interaction within the family system.

The Morris family includes two adolescents: their daughter, Rose, in high school, and their son, George, in junior high school. The family tells Mr. Gonzales that they have had difficulty feeling accepted by grandparents and relatives on both sides of the family. The African American grandparents and relatives live across the continent on the East Coast; therefore distance and a lack of money for travel have been deterrents to developing close relationships with the African American side of the family. Mrs. Morris says that her family never really accepted her marrying someone as dark-skinned as Mr. Morris. Mrs. Morris's mother usually visits when Mr. Morris is at work. There have been numerous times when cousins have made fun of Rose's dark skin. Her maternal grandmother told her to not play outside in the sun so much because it makes her skin even darker.

It is important to assess the way the interracial family deals with unexpected crises that occur during the family life cycle to gain clues about who, or what group, does (or does not) serve as a support system for the interracial family (Faulkner & Kich, 1983). Other interracial families often provide the support that may be missing from the extended family.

Earlier this year, Mr. Morris's brother was killed in a car accident in Florida. Mr. Morris did not go to the funeral because of the cost of the trip. At this time the Morris family received little support from the family of Rose's mother. Biracial Mexican American/African American neighbors had the family over for dinner after that crisis occurred.

Gibbs (1987) stresses the importance of assessing parental and family attitudes toward the interracial status of the family. Some parents act as if society is color blind and minimize any problems that the family's mixed heritage may present. Some parents give mixed messages to their children about their physical appearance. Other parents do little or nothing to talk with their children about the racial heritages of the family.

Mr. Morris tells Mr. Gonzales that they have difficulty talking about their interracial situation. Rose's mother says that she tells Rose how pretty she is with her dark curly hair, but admits that she, too, encourages Rose to keep out of the sun to try to lighten her skin coloring.

The assessment of *intimacy and boundaries* can be a test of the counselor's awareness of the impact of culture on who or what unit (the individual or the family) are made central to decision making and the way that different cultures can have an impact on the development of boundaries in a family. In the interracial family, problems may arise because individual members do not understand or respect these differences. Mr. Gonzales will look for the flexibility or rigidity of family rules, styles of communication, and ways of solving problems in assessing these aspects of intimacy and boundaries. He has already noted that Mrs. Morris seems to wait for her husband to talk first before she speaks, and that Rose and George are inconsistent in the way they interact with their mother and father, sometimes coming on strong and sometimes deferring to their parents.

A specific area for Mr. Gonzales to assess is the way that the Morris family traditionally copes when they are faced with challenges or negation. He will look for responses and behaviors that the family has developed that maintain intimacy and family boundaries. Mr. Gonzales will ask the Morris family how they have responded to staring or questions such as "Where did you get these children?" or "Whose children are these?" He will pay special attention to how various members of the family answer these questions, which family member responds first, and what consensus or disagreements may surface. Mr. Gonzales will help the family work out a system of positive responses to these intrusions in order to reinforce their pride and the boundaries in their interracial family (Faulkner & Kich, 1983).

Sometimes mutual protection within the interracial family can lead to unhealthy enmeshment or disengagement. Kahn (1993) emphasizes the importance of process in family therapy and states: "Issues such as overinvolvement, enmeshment, disengagement, and diffusion still require working with and realigning family boundaries and subsystems" (p. 112). Mr. Gonzales suspects that some of these behaviors may be maintaining an unhealthy Morris family atmosphere, but he wants to watch the family interaction more carefully before intervening to help the family make needed changes.

Interracial children's responses are of particular importance in assessment because interracial children have a unique identity that combines the racial identities of both parents. In manifesting this unique identity, children sometimes display negative feelings because they are the ones who have to deal with society's reactions to their appearance and ambiguous status. If the parents have unresolved issues of acceptance of their own racial identities and have not been open in helping their children with racial exploration, this may impede the children's racial identity development (Faulkner & Kich, 1983). As noted in the previous section, the counselor has observed the need to work with the Morris family on issues of interracial identity.

Mr. Gonzales will capitalize on his knowledge of racial identity development in interracial children and adolescents in work with the Morris family. He plans to talk with them about the patterns of racial identity development that often occur in interracial children (such as difficulty in knowing what to call themselves and stages of sequential ambivalence toward the racial heritages of their parents). All family members will be asked what they remember about either of these identity development phases.

Rose and George will be encouraged to talk about problems they are currently experiencing that may be related to their interracial identity. It is especially important for the parents to realize the pressures that peers are putting on both Rose and George to choose one racial identity. Mr. Gonzales hopes that Rose and George will share how lonely they are and will talk about peer pressures to choose one identity. Assessment of the way that Rose and George interact with their parents during discussion of the interracial identity development phases will give Mr. Gonzales clues as to how the family functions in discussing racial identity issues.

Engagement of the Interracial Family. In order to be effective in counseling with an interracial family, the counselor must engage the family in a working relationship. Faulkner and Kich (1983) suggest that use of four techniques or concepts will aid the counselor in successfully engaging the interracial family: *joining and self-disclosure, clarification about questions, family self-identification*, and *hierarchy and culture*. In reality, Mr. Gonzales has used many of these techniques in the assessment process just described.

Joining and self-disclosure are essential in developing a working relationship with an interracial family. Joining is the process of forming a connectedness with the family while maintaining the separateness needed to do therapy. Self-disclosure is a critical aspect of joining but must be carried out in a culturally sensitive way. In the case of the Morris family, Mr. Gonzales must not attempt to join with the Morris family on the basis that he shares Mexican American group membership with Mrs. Morris because this may alienate other Morris family members (Baptiste, 1990). Instead, he may begin joining with them by noting that he and his wife also have a daughter in high school and a son in junior high.

Kahn (1993) sees joining with each family member as the first step in transcultural family therapy and a step that takes place during every session. In the joining process, it is important to remember the uniqueness of each individual within each culture group and to not stereotype individuals on the basis of their culture(s). During the initial session, however, counselors may want to remember cultural influences on who to speak to first in the joining process in case the family abides by the traditional values of their culture.

Counselors trained in cross-cultural therapy are aware of the importance of self-disclosure in relationship development (Sue & Sue, 1990). It may be essential for the counselor to self-disclose first before she or he can expect clients of different cultures to self-disclose. "Giving advice or suggestions, interpreting, and telling the client how you, the counselor, feel are really acts of counselor self-disclosure" (Sue & Sue, 1990, p. 71).

The counselor may share personal experiences and thus model open discussion about topics that are relevant to work with the interracial family, but the focus must be kept on the family that has come for counseling. It is appropriate to ask the family members to help the counselor understand how they deal with issues that interracial families face. One such issue on which Mr. Gonzales might ask for input would be how they complete race category questions on their children's enrollment blanks when the blanks do not offer the option of showing that the child has more than one racial heritage.

The process of *clarifications about questions* involves explaining to the family why certain questions are asked and why the counselor needs information on racial/ethnic distinctions in the answers to questions. It can help to acknowledge that it is not always easy to talk openly about some of the differences that will become apparent during the counseling sessions. The counselor helps families recognize the importance of sharing and discussing different perspectives of each family member.

Some questions asked in counseling with interracial families require special sensitivity so as to reduce any perceived threat or intimidation. Faulkner and Kich (1983) note that the question of how or where the couple met could be misinterpreted and recommend that the question be phrased "When did you meet?" (p. 85). Wording the question this way usually leads to the same type of information in a less threatening way. Mr. Gonzales asked Mr. and Mrs. Morris when they met. Both responded with animation, telling how they met at a community gathering for soldiers stationed at a nearby military base 18 years ago. Proper sensitivity in asking and clarifying questions is particularly important in gathering information related to the family life cycles discussed in the previous section. Counselor use of sensitive clarifications serves as a model for families to use in their own verbal interactions.

Information from *family self-identification* can be some of the most important data obtained in the process of engaging the interracial family. Counselor self-disclosure on family self-identification is a way to model and join the family in its self-identification. The counselor then asks the family to share how they identify or label themselves. The answers that the family presents give the counselor "the opportunity to assess ego and family intimacy strengths" (Faulkner & Kich, 1983, p. 86). Their responses also help the counselor understand if the family is recognizing all of the family's racial heritages and if they have resolved issues of loss or rejection because of their interracial status. When Mr. Gonzales asked the Morrises how they identify themselves, the parents stated that they just considered themselves good Americans. Rose responded that she calls herself a "Heinz 57"; George said he just tells people to "bug off" when he gets asked about his racial identity.

Counselor recognition of *hierarchy and culture* are important in the engagement process. Knowledge of the cultural impact on the interracial family's style of interacting and parenting can be obtained during the counseling sessions. The importance of respecting cultural influences on who to speak to first in the joining process was mentioned earlier. This is an example of hierarchy and culture. When extended family members are present, issues of hierarchical roles may be of special importance in facilitating the family sessions.

Race and culture may influence a variety of family roles and interactions, such as power dispersion among family members, nurture and discipline responsibilities, habitual communication patterns, and expectations of family members according to gender, age, and family position. Mr. Gonzales can help the Morris family members look at the way they interact in their discussion of problems that they bring to the session, respecting the impact of culture on expectations for hierarchy.

Faulkner and Kich (1983) note that loyalty dilemmas and attempts to resolve loyalty issues may be basic areas of conflict for interracial families. Loyalty dilemmas brought by the interracial family members sometimes indicate conflicts the interracial family has faced in being accepted by the extended family or the community. Kich (1982) found that some Asian communities are very vocal about loss of traditional Asian values in Asian interracial marriage. Graham's 1995 listing of six objections that some Black people have to interracial coupling is another example of loyalty issues that a cross-racially married Black person and her or his spouse and family might bring to family counseling.

Mr. Gonzales has noted that loyalty issues are present for the Morris family. Both Mr. and Mrs. Morris are proud of their racial heritages; neither wants to give up this pride. Mr. Morris has said that he does not understand why Mrs. Morris can't just accept the fact that their kids are Black because that is the way that everyone else sees them. Rose says she wants to claim all three heritages. Although George glibly says, "It doesn't matter to me," Mr. Gonzales needs to look for George's true feelings.

Issues Identification for Future Family Counseling Sessions. During the process of assessment and engagement of the family it will be important for Mr. Gonzales to listen for recurring themes that give clues as to issues on which the family wants help. One such theme that he has heard is the issue of how Rose and George should identify themselves racially and how the family as a unit identifies itself. Another theme is that of helping Rose be a better student "like she used to be." Concurrently Mr. Gonzales will listen for strengths of the family. He has noticed that perseverance seems to be a strength for all of them. Mr. Morris has worked at his job as an auto mechanic for years and is proud of the respect he has gained for this skill. Mr. Gonzales has also noticed that the family seems determined to help Rose and continues coming for counseling. Mrs. Morris prides herself in being a good wife and mother. Rose and George take pride in having perfect attendance records at their respective schools.

Feedback to the Morris family has included both family strengths and issues that the counselor has heard. Mr. Gonzales complimented the family on their perseverance and on the special pride each family member has shown. He told them that it sounds as if they may need help on discussing and deciding on a common racial identification term for the family. Mr. Gonzales also asks them if they could all work together to decide when and how to react to overt acts of prejudice and racism.

As counselor, Mr. Gonzales negotiates with the family regarding issues on which they will commit to work. The family decides that they would like to work first on the issue of racial identity. Then they will tackle ways to respond to prejudice and racism. In this way the Morris family is involved in developing goals and selecting the issues to which they will give their first and subsequent attention. Mr. Gonzales has explained to the family that counseling involves work on these issues both in and out of the counseling sessions.

Psychoeducational Counselor Roles With Interracial Families

Much of the counselor's work with interracial families is in the psychoeducational realm (Poston, 1990). There is a strong need for interracial families to engage in frequent discussions of racial and ethnic identity issues. Counselors can help by modeling these discussions in family counseling sessions, by helping the family to find a convenient time to meet and discuss issues at home, and by giving the family assignments that will engage them in collective efforts (Gibbs & Hines, 1992). Mr. Gonzales has helped the Morris family find a time that they can gather each week for a discussion of family issues. The time on which they agreed is immediately after dinner on Tuesday evening.

Gibbs (1989) also recommends involving the interracial family in collective efforts that will build both family pride and the self-esteem of individual family members. She encourages family participation in recreational activities centered around ethnic themes, interracial activities that are church-based, and political activities that enhance the status of the minority heritage(s) of interracial families. The Morris family is looking for area ethnic events that celebrate all three of their heritages: African American, Mexican American, and Native American Navajo Nation. They seem excited about doing more to participate in ethnic celebrations. The family shares a common religious heritage, Catholicism.

The following are some issues faced by interracial families that may be addressed through counselor use of a combination of psychodynamic and educational skills: (a) helping the family to recognize

both (or all) of their racial/ethnic identities, (b) assisting parents to
help their children and adolescents develop a positive biracial/inter-
racial identity, and (c) helping the family to address discrimination
and racism. These are broad and overlapping areas. Work with any
one of these issues can easily "spill over" into work with the others.
Information obtained through the assessment and engagement processes just described will provide the counselor with a starting base
for work in any of these areas. The discussions that follow are based
on the assumption that the counselor and the family have agreed to
work on these areas.

Helping the Family Recognize Both (or All) of Their Racial/Ethnic Identities

A host of authors underscore the importance of family nurturance of
all racial heritages of the interracial child so that the child develops
a positive interracial identity (e.g., Brandell, 1988; Brody, 1984;
Chen, 1984; Gibbs, 1987, 1989; Gibbs & Hines, 1992; Hall, 1980;
Lyles et al., 1985; McRoy & Freeman, 1986; Poston, 1990, Poussaint, 1984; Root, 1990, 1992c, 1994; Spivey, 1984; Wardle, 1990,
1992a).

Strengthening the interracial family's positive feelings about their
racial heritages may involve activities such as interviewing older
family members to learn more about the family's history and making
family trees. Family history can also be researched from old photograph albums, historic documents possessed by the family, and legal
records at local court houses and registries (as described in Chapter
5). Wolfman's book, *Do People Grow on Family Trees? Genealogy for
Kids & Other Beginners* (1991) is also appropriate for family use. Mr.
Gonzales is encouraging the Morris family to get involved in such
an effort and has let them borrow Wolfman's book.

In gathering this historic information, the Morris family should
be encouraged to look for strengths of their ancestors. If children or
teenagers have already been involved in researching the family's history, this is an ideal time to have them share their work with the
rest of the family. At Cortez High School Rose has begun this
research in her sophomore English class. She seems excited about

talking with her family about what she has already learned. George is beginning to show interest in studying family genealogy.

Because direct contact with some older members of the Morris family is not possible, there are other methods that the family can use to learn about their racial history and culture. There are now many printed and media sources of information on people and cultures of the world (e.g., encyclopedias of culture, biographies, travel books, and videos). Rose is busy perusing the encyclopedias of culture at both the high school and local libraries. She is also looking for stories of heroes, pioneers, and leaders from the racial groups represented by her family and will share this information in family meetings and with Mr. Gonzales. Mr. Gonzales anticipates that this will increase the family's pride in their racial roots.

The counselor encourages parents to expand and continue to give clear and positive racial information to the family (Adler, 1987). Gibbs (1987) notes that parents may need to "confront their own racial attitudes so that they can give clear, consistent, and positive feedback to their children about both sides of their racial heritage" (p. 275). Mr. Gonzales has involved Mr. and Mrs. Morris in discussing their attitudes and their perceptions of their own and each other's racial heritages. This discussion seemed to clear misunderstandings that existed with both parents. Rose and George have reported that their parents seem more open to discuss racial matters since the session in which Mr. Gonzales helped the parents come to a broader understanding.

Assisting Parents to Help Their Children and Adolescents Develop a Biracial/Interracial Identity

The activities described in the previous section are basic to developing positive biracial/interracial identities. Participating in a multicultural lifestyle that exposes children and adolescents to a variety of cultural and ethnic role models, institutions, and activities also helps interracial youth become comfortable in a wide variety of situations (Gibbs & Hines, 1992).

As noted in the section on assessment of racial identity development of the family's offspring, the counselor can inform parents of current knowledge of the stages and phases that biracial/interracial children and adolescents experience in attaining this identity (see Chapters 4 and 5). Mr. Gonzales included this information in an early family counseling session. Rose and George report that their parents now seem more willing to listen when they share experiences that happen at school.

The Morris family is discussing how each member self-labels racially in their Tuesday night family meetings. Mr. Gonzales continues to model leadership of these discussions and show family members how to show respect for the self-label choices of each individual. The family is working on selecting a racial self-label that both of the parents and Rose and George can use with comfort.

Kich (1982) underscores the importance of parental participation in development of their children's interracial self-concept. "Parents, by providing their children the structure and the words that help them make sense of their experiences as they develop their self-concept and self-esteem, play a crucial role in the lives of biracial children during this early stage" (Kich, 1992, p. 308).

Helping the Family Address Discrimination and Racism

Discrimination and racism are issues that interracial children and adolescents will face no matter how much parents may try to protect them (Shackford, 1984). The family that has not involved their children in discussions of discrimination and racism may find it awkward to begin this process. The use of books as a basis for family discussion can help smooth the transition to talking about issues of discrimination and racism. Even though Rose and George are older than the children in Rosenberg's book, *Living in Two Worlds* (1986), the family might still find it useful because the children in this book talk about racism and discrimination. Gay's *The Rainbow Effect: Interracial Families* (1987) may be more appropriate for the Morris family to use as a basis of discussion because it includes chapters telling the stories of interracial families that include adolescents. Other books are listed in Appendix B, Interracial Books and Stories.

Mr. Gonzales could have the family members share with him their reactions to stories about interracial families.

When a family is open to discuss discrimination and racism, even young children have much to share about interactions with other children or adults. Counselors model discussions of discrimination and racism during counseling sessions. Families can learn how to show empathy for hurt and angry feelings. However, steps beyond recognizing feelings are needed to help reduce or eliminate the discrimination.

Clarification of the "What?," "When?," and "How?" are often pertinent because it is easy for children to learn to get attention by playing the victim role. Once it is clear that discrimination did occur, the family has choices of routes that they can take. Suggestions for addressing racism in the family follow.

Brown (1987) suggests teaching survival skills to children of Black/White intermarriages to prepare them for racial slurs and recommends that the Black parent be made responsible for preparing her or his biracial child for these interactions because the Black parent has experienced similar situations. Spickard (1989) noted that in Black/Japanese families the Black parent assumed the responsibilities for preparing the children for prejudice and racism. Mr. Gonzales will explore what Mr. and Mrs. Morris have done to educate their children on how to handle racist incidents.

Miller and Miller (1990) state that socialization processes in African American families are inadequately described in the psychological literature and that literature on parenting issues of Black/White families is almost nonexistent. The Millers delineate Boykin and Tom's "Triple Quandary" paradigm that explains how African American parents help their children to integrate values of three competing systems: "majority values, African-American culture, and a minority group agenda" (Miller & Miller, 1990, p. 171). These authors believe that biracial Black/White families face similar challenges and can profit from learning these coping style dimensions. Mr. Gonzales may adapt the Triple Quandary model of four coping styles for discussion with the interracial Morris family.

1. The first dimension is *active-passive*. Offering sympathy only to the interracial child who comes home and reports being called a

"White Nigger" or a "mongrel" is passive coping. Calling the school or the parent of the offending peer to discuss the incident involves the active dimension.

2. *System-engagement versus system-disengagement* is related to balancing work in mainstream institutions such as the school P.T.A. and the family's regular support groups such as churches or social clubs to bring about changes.

3. *System-maintenance and system-change* is similar to system-engagement and system-disengagement. Parents model successful negotiation of mainstream institutions while showing pride and skills in fighting structural racism in the institutions.

4. The fourth dimension, *system-blame versus personal blame* addresses whether children are socialized "to believe that the status of people of color is a function of systems that support and maintain discrimination as opposed to viewing these as the flaws and failure of minority people" (Miller & Miller, 1990, p. 173).

Ponterotto (1991) suggests that family counseling focus on prejudice awareness and prevention: "If we can assume that family, particularly parents and older siblings, play a pivotal role teaching prejudice to children, then family counseling may provide effective avenues for attitude change" (p. 223). Ponterotto (1991) and Ponterotto and Pedersen (1993) present a theoretical basis for prejudice prevention and outline roles and activities for counselors to use with individuals and groups. They note that family counseling literature has not addressed prejudice awareness prevention. It appears that this is virgin territory for counselors working with interracial families. Mr. Gonzales and Mr. Wood are meeting to discuss working together to deliver a developmental prejudice prevention program at the junior and senior high schools and through the local mental health agency.

Other Counselor Roles With Interracial Families

The use of concepts from the structural family therapy approach, the extended family system paradigm, and experiential family systems therapy in transcultural family counseling are delineated by Kahn (1993). Two of the family counseling models presented by Kahn with modifications for transcultural counseling are especially appropriate for counselor use with interracial families. A few concepts from these two models with additional modifications for application to interracial families are highlighted here. Readers interested in more details are referred to Kahn (1993). Also included in this section is Baptiste's discussion of the use of a systems approach with interracial stepfamilies and an introduction to a model for cross-cultural couples counseling.

Structural Family Therapy Concepts for Use With Interracial Families

Structural family therapy capitalizes on the process of family therapy and "provides a theoretical framework that guides counselors' interventions through consistent strategies of treatment that in turn reduce the need to use specific techniques for various occasions" (Kahn, 1993, p. 111). The concepts of *structure, subsystems,* and *boundaries* are of particular value in understanding and identifying family interaction issues. Mr. Gonzales will review these concepts as they relate to his work with the Morris family.

Structure is the organized pattern of interactions used by the family. In the interracial family the cultures of both parents may influence the structure. Counselors are alerted to look carefully for influences of the cultures of both parents on the family structure patterns that occur in family interactions.

As noted earlier, Mr. Gonzales has already seen cultural influences on verbal interactions in the Morris family. He has helped the family realize these cultural influences and they are deciding if any of these interactions need to be changed.

Subsystems are "the primary building blocks of the family" (Kahn, 1993, p. 112). Each family member is a subsystem of the family and these subsystems join to form additional family systems. Cultural influences may have an impact on how the subsystems are formed (by generation, gender, or interests). Subsystems are both overt and covert. Family counselors looks especially for covert subsystems that influence family interaction. Studying the interracial Morris family subsystems has been an extra challenge for Mr. Gonzales because of the possible influence of at least three cultures on covert subsystems.

Boundaries have already been recognized in the section on assessment. Boundaries are invisible and they surround each individual and subsystem of the family. Kahn notes that boundaries serve to protect subsystems in the family. They can be "rigid or diffuse and create disengagement or enmeshment between various family members" (Kahn, 1993, p. 112). The generational boundary in an interracial family is an important one to observe because it may be different for each parent. As noted earlier, definitions of enmeshment take on new meanings in cross-cultural therapy. Mr. Gonzales should use much cultural sensitivity in working to realign boundaries in the interracial Morris family.

Kahn sees structural family therapy as appropriate in transcultural counseling because it focuses on process and work in restructuring family interactions rather than on emotions and content. Even in the single-parent interracial family there may be evidence of the impact of both parents on family structure unless the parents separated when children were very young and the children have had little or no contact with the extended family of the absent parent. Mr. Gonzales recognizes that cultural sensitivity in restructuring of family interactions is critical to his success with counseling the Morris family.

Bowen's Extended Family System Paradigm and Techniques

Although Bowen is concerned about the multigenerational family, he usually works with individuals or couples. One of Bowen's major concepts is that of triangulations within families. Therapy is viewed as a lifelong process of self-discovery. Clients are given tools to travel back to their family of origin to differentiate the self. "Differentiation is a process of becoming independent of, but still in contact with, the family of origin, both nuclear and extended" (Kahn, 1993, p. 117). The eight interlocking concepts of Bowen's extended family system theory are: *emotional triangles, differentiation of self, nuclear family emotional system, family projection process, multigenerational projection system, influence of sibling position, emotional cutoff,* and *societal regressions.*

Bowen believes that emotional triangles are formed soon after couples begin living together because two-person relationships are difficult to maintain on a stable basis. A third person, object, or situation is pulled in to relieve stress. If a child is present, the child becomes the focus of attention. Another alternative is for one member of the couple to begin to put much focus on her or his work. When the third person, object, or situation receives the attention, triangulation occurs. The stress is removed but the original issue is not resolved.

Kahn notes that triangulation occurs in families worldwide, but that culture can dictate how triangles are formed and which family member plays major roles. "In a family with a different cultural perspective it may not be easy to identify the part of the triangle that affects the marital couple the most . . . or to develop strategies for effectively detriangulating the couple without offending their cultural mores or values" (Kahn, 1993, p. 118). Mr. Gonzales will teach the Morris family about triangulation and how they can go back to their extended families and detriangulate themselves to become more differentiated. He may need to explore possible cultural influences on triangulation and differentiation. The three major cultures in the interracial Morris family can increase the complexities of using this approach.

Mr. Gonzales already has hunches about possible triangulation that has occurred (Mr. Morris spending so much time away from home at work and Mrs. Morris spending much time with her mother while Mr. Morris is at work and the children are in school) or is occurring (focus on Rose as the one with all of the problems). He is waiting to see what insight the Morris family can develop on their own before acting on his hunches.

The nuclear family emotional system assumes that patterns of previous generations will be repeated in the current family. If spouses have little differentiation from their families of origin, fusion can occur within the marriage. Future problems within a family can be predicted by the degree of fusion in a marriage. Mr. Gonzales will look closely at Mrs. Morris's possible fusion with her mother.

The family projection process occurs because parents emotionally transfer their lack of differentiation and immaturity to their children.

If there is emotional distance between a couple, one parent may fuse with a child through an overly dependent bond or through conflict. The child with whom the parent fuses often suffers emotionally; this, in turn, leads to more dysfunctional family behavior. Mr. Gonzales will study the Morris family to see if either the father or mother have developed an overly dependent bond or an ongoing conflict with one of their children.

The multigenerational transmission process is the way that family problems are transferred from generation to generation. Bowen believes that the dysfunction of an identified patient is the result of at least a three-generational transmission. Including extended family members in treatment can be very beneficial to understand and treat family dysfunction. In interracial families where families of origin may be estranged, it may be an extra challenge to get the information needed. Mr. Gonzales is aware that it is impossible to get the extended family of Mr. Morris involved in therapy because they live so far away. After additional work with the Morris nuclear family, he may want to involve Mrs. Morris's parents in the family counseling.

Sibling position is especially important for Mr. Gonzales to study in the Morris family because there may be the influence of three cultures on both hierarchy and sibling position. Cultural perspectives of both parents on birth order are needed by the interracial family counselor to deliver culturally sensitive counseling. Mr. Gonzales has noticed differences between the perspectives of Mr. and Mrs. Morris on both hierarchy and sibling position. Mrs. Morris has placed emphasis on George as the child who should assume leadership because he is male. Mr. Morris does not see why this is such a big deal.

"Emotional cutoff indicates that people are emotionally or physically cut off from their parents to start a new life with their peer generation" (Kahn, 1993, p. 120). When individuals abruptly abandon their families of origin or never break emotional ties with their families, problems occur. Emotional cutoff sometimes results when people move long distances from their families. Mr. Gonzales may need to use creative measures to assist the Morris family because he believes they may be suffering emotional cutoff because of distance from Mr. Morris's family. On the other hand, Mr. Gonzales wants to look very closely at the relationship Mrs. Morris has with her family because he realizes that what looks like enmeshment may not be enmeshment in the Mexican American and Navajo cultures.

Mr. Gonzales has much to keep in mind in the sessions in which he will work with the Morris family. Some of the many family therapy techniques that he is considering for use in these sessions are link therapy, the fishbowl technique, family sculpting, family drawing, role playing, auxiliary ego, homework assignments, and reframing or relabeling (Kahn, 1993). Mr. Gonzales is optimistic that the Morris family will continue to cooperate and realize the benefits from family counseling.

Baptiste's Suggestions for Counseling Interracial Stepfamilies

Baptiste (1984) addresses the challenges of marriage and family therapy with racially/culturally intermarried stepfamilies. The addition of the "step" component further compounds issues for interracial families. The therapist who is successful with interracial stepfamilies will need to be very knowledgeable in work with stepfamilies as well as in work with interracial families. Baptiste recommends the use of a systems approach that incorporates behavioral techniques. The first phase focuses on understanding the family system. Behavioral approaches are used in the second phase to "change maladaptive behavior through 'doing' " (Baptiste, 1984, p. 378). Other goals are directed toward helping members of the interracial stepfamily clarify their relationships in the family, understand and clarify their own family interactions and behaviors, and improve family communication.

Cross-Cultural Couples Counseling

Counselors working with interracial couples and not their families might find the article, "Cross-cultural Couples Counseling: A Developmental, Psychoeducational Intervention," by Ibrahim and Schroeder (1990) helpful. Detailed information is included on assessing world views, family life cycle issues, relationship issues, cultural knowledge, and cross-cultural skills. After assessment, the paradigm includes a psychoeducational intervention "to enhance the couple's ability to actively understand their issues and to learn to resolve them, while accepting one another as 'cultural beings' " (Ibrahim & Schroeder, 1990, p. 202).

Special Considerations for Counseling With Families That Have Become Interracial Through Cross-Racial Adoption or Cross-Racial Foster Home Placement

Chapters 4 and 5 included discussions of special considerations for counseling interracial children and adolescents in adoptive or foster homes. Details of research reported in the 1983 book by McRoy and Zurcher, *Transracial and Inracial Adoptees: The Adolescent Years*, are given in Chapter 5 and will not be repeated in this chapter. Findings that have implications for counselor work with adoptive parents will be underscored.

Implications for Family Counseling From the McRoy and Zurcher Research

McRoy and Zurcher (1983) found that transracially adopted Black (and Black/White) adolescents were somewhat reluctant to discuss racist incidents with their White adoptive parents. This finding supports the need for counselors to model the discussion of racist incidents in counseling sessions with cross-racial adoptive families. Counselors can educate White parents on ways to help their transracially adopted children deal with prejudice, discrimination, and racism.

A second finding of the McRoy and Zurcher research was that Black children adopted into White homes sometimes needed more help in learning about their Black heritage. If counselors note that this is true in their assessment of the adoptive family, they can give extra emphasis to the importance of parental involvement in helping adopted children learn about their racial heritages.

Transracial adoptees living in White neighborhoods and attending predominantly White schools in the McRoy and Zurcher study experienced some teasing, heckling, and staring in their neighborhoods and at school. Counselors working with transracial adoptive parents can assess if their adoptees are being discriminated against in this way and do necessary follow-up work with the families.

Another issue that may need special attention in counseling with transracially adoptive families is how the family defines itself racially and how the adoptive child or children self-define racially. Counselor assistance with discussion of racial self-definitions may be of great value to the family.

Controversy Over Transracial Adoption

For more than two decades transracial adoption in the United States has been restricted for African American and interracial children with African American heritage. Because the transracial adoption issue has received much attention, it is important for counselors to be aware of the history and current status of this controversy. A few highlights are included here. Counselors are encouraged to follow the. latest legal interpretations of this issue in order to best serve families who have adopted transracially or are in the process of transracial adoption.

The strongest deterrent to transracial adoption occurred in 1972 when the National Association of Black Social Workers (NABSW) went on record as unconditionally opposed to transracial adoption of Black and biracial Black/White children. Since that time the NABSW has continued to speak out against transracial adoption and has had a pervasive impact on how social workers in the United States implement placement of Black and Black/White children in adoptive homes. As a result, a large of number of adoptable children wait for years to be placed in same-race homes. In April 1995 the Department of Health and Human Services distributed new guidelines for inter-racial adoption to implement the Multiethnic Placement Act passed by Congress in October 1994. The Multiethnic Placement Act of 1994 states that race cannot be the primary factor in placing children for adoption.

The issue of trans- or cross-racial adoption has been given much attention in the recent press (e.g., Burrell, 1995; Evans, 1993; Havemann, 1995; Holmes, 1995; Melina, 1990; Weiss, 1994;

Wheeler, 1993). In the spring of 1995 lawsuits were filed in Texas and in Tennessee to "prevent children from spending months or years in foster care when adults of different races are willing to adopt them" (Burrell, 1995, p. 5B).

Longitudinal Research of Transracial Adoption by Simon and Associates

The longitudinal research of transracial adoption by Simon and associates as reported most recently in *The Case for Transracial Adoption* (Simon, Alstein, & Melli, 1994) and in *Adoption, Race, and Identity: From Infancy through Adolescence* (Simon & Alstein, 1992) is worthy of review. In both books the authors give detailed coverage of the history of adoption in the United States, the agencies and regulations that have controlled transracial adoption, and results of research of transracial adoption since the early 1970s.

Simon and associates began their studies of families that adopted transracially in 1972. The adoptive parents and their children participated in in-depth interviews to gather a wide variety of information. Three follow-up studies were conducted of the original group (in 1979, 1984, and 1991), and therefore the most recent report (Simon et al., 1994) covers a 20-year period. Major findings of the longitudinal research are reported under these headings in the 1994 report: Parent Socioeconomic Characteristics; Birth and Adoption Patterns; Neighborhoods, Schools, and Friends; The Adoption Experience; The Parents' Reactions; and The Children's Reactions.

In their concluding remarks Simon et al. (1994) state that the outcomes of their research are basically positive and do not support the warnings of the NABSW that transracially adopted children will grow up confused about their racial identity. The authors are very concerned that thousands of Black children continue to be kept in institutions and foster home care while waiting for same-race placement. In their "Policy Recommendations" chapter, Simon et al. recommend that more extensive consideration and support be given to subsidized adoption, especially to foster parents who adopt children that have been in their care. The authors believe that this will increase the probability that minority foster parents will become adoptive parents. Simon et al. (1994) close their book with this plea:

> Move the thousands of children who are available for adoption out of the institutions and out of their temporary foster placement, and into permanent homes! Apply the standard *best interest of the child* as the first and foremost criterion in child placement! Make the move without regard to race! (p. 116)

Wardle's Recommendations for Meeting the Needs of Transracially Adopted Children

Wardle, who was cited several times in recommendations for serving the needs of interracial children in schools and daycare programs in Chapter 5, went on record as a strong supporter of adoption across races in 1992. His article, "Transracial and Interracial Adoption: The Myth of Cultural Genocide," addresses controversial adoption issues. He lists 11 recommendations to parents involved in transracial adoption. Wardle (1992b) summarizes his viewpoints:

> Research shows that White parents who raise their minority, adopted children with a clear, healthy sense of their minority, adopted heritage, expose them to a variety of people, and adjust their lifestyle to respond to the needs of their children, raise mature, well-adjusted people. . . . But the White family that adopts transracially must be prepared to challenge a society (including institutions and some professionals) who are at best insensitive to their families, and at worst, hostile. (p. 31)

Internationally Adopted Children

One of the consequences of the ongoing controversy over transracial adoption is that there is a shortage of babies and children that are adoptable in the United States This has led to an increase in international adoptions.

For counselors working with families that have adopted internationally, two journal articles may be insightful (Myer & James, 1989; Ramos, 1990). Myer and James recommend that school counselors counsel the children individually and serve in a consultant capacity with adoptive parents and school staff. Ramos notes that international adoption is a middle-class phenomenon because of the expenses involved. She views adoptive parents as excellent sources of information about their children and about adoption issues because many are involved in networks to share information.

Summary

This chapter has given an overview of topics related to counseling with interracial families. After reiterating the need for counselor self-examination of biases, issues that interracial families may bring to counseling were discussed. Counselor roles in working with interracial families were reviewed through applying concepts and techniques to work with a hypothetical interracial African American/ Mexican American/Native American Navajo family. The chapter closed with a section on counseling with families that have become interracial through cross-racial adoption.

8

Challenges to Move Beyond the "Other" Status

This book was written to promote counselor interest in a population that has received minimal attention by the counseling profession. Producing the manuscript has involved integrating information from other social sciences, clinical observations, and the popular press with the limited professional literature on counseling interracial individuals and families. It is hoped that the book will serve as a "springboard" for counseling theory building and research and lead to expansion of a professional knowledge base of appropriate interracial counseling interventions.

Readers have been introduced to the sociopolitical history and changing societal perceptions of mixed-race people in the United States. Numerous research investigations of biracial/interracial identity development have been reported. From the research reports and from a host of personal accounts from interracial persons in the popular press, patterns of strengths and needs are emerging. Counselor roles have been suggested for helping interracial people meet these needs. Much remains to be done in developing appropriate interracial counseling interventions. Counselors have the potential to serve as strong allies in interracial people's quest for identity and respect.

Chapter 8 addresses the challenges, the "To Dos," for counselor roles with interracial people. It will underscore some of the many challenges that lie ahead for counseling professionals to "stand and serve" the unique interracial population. Many of the "To Dos" will require counselors to move out and work beyond the confines of their private offices. Being agents of change in the lives of others involves taking an active role in the social systems in which our clients live. Counselors can become active in political action groups to change the oppression that interracial people experience.

Challenges discussed in this chapter are not listed in hierarchical order. Again, as in so many other topics addressed in this book, there is overlap. Work to change one challenge may have an effect on other challenges.

Challenge I

Legitimize an Identity for Interracial People

In an ideal world, racial labels or categories are not needed; however, we do not live in an ideal world. The United States is a country that places much importance on racial categories; public policy decisions and compliance with legislation often require racial enumeration. "At a political level, race is in the service of economic and social privilege" (Root, 1992d, p. 4). A clear category is needed for mixed-race people to indicate their interracial status.

At present two alternatives exist for interracial people in "Please check one" racial registrations. One alternative is to deny half (or more) of their racial heritage and check one category. The second alternative is to check "Other." The "Other" category for racial identity is viewed negatively by most multiracial people because it leaves them raceless and "between and betwixt." As long as people feel they are without a racial identity or that they are denying part of themselves, there is a high probability that they will feel marginal (Thornton, 1983). The process of naming all of oneself has an empowering effect because it validates one's existence and makes the person visible (Root, 1992d). Having a clear identity gives the individual a "self-knowledge of one's coherence and authenticity" (Hoare, 1991, p. 47).

To help bring about the changes needed to legitimize an identity for interracial people, it will be important for counselors to work with this group as well as with people of color community groups that may have reservations about supporting a separate identity for interracial people. Becoming active and visible in community interest groups may be a first step. Volunteering to present educational sessions is another possibility. With some groups, counselors will have the opportunity to use their skills of group facilitation and conflict resolution to help the people involved recognize and support a separate identity for interracial persons.

As Brown (1995), Jacobs (1992), Root (1990, 1992d), and many other authors cited in this book have stated, interracial people need both legal and social sanctions to support an interracial self-identification. Not only must institutions at all levels acknowledge and make legitimate their interracial or multiracial status, but society needs to change to accept these people as a new group to be respected and celebrated. Again, counselors have a golden opportunity to work in psychoeducational roles and in change agent roles to gain societal support for interracial people. The popular press is giving attention to the delimiting effect of the government's four racial categories on interracial people (e.g., Begley, 1995; Sandor, 1994). Counselors might capitalize on popular press information to "join" their groups and lead discussions and critiques of these press reports. Societal support of interracial status is needed to reduce the emotional turmoil that mixed-race people now experience in declaring their racial identity (Brown, 1995).

Challenge 2

Help Interracial People Find Role Models and People With Whom They Can Identify

The lack of role models to serve as "a clear racial reference group" (Root, 1990, p. 188) has made it difficult for interracial people to gain a positive multiracial identity. Many of the people interviewed by Funderburg (1994) spoke of the dearth of role models and of people who truly understand the Black/White biracial perspective. The intrapersonal conflicts suffered by interracial people can never be completely understood by parents or monoracial friends.

One avenue that can provide opportunities to meet interracial role models is through interracial support groups. The counselor can help locate area support groups for interracial clients. If none are available, the counselor can initiate steps to start such a group.

Interracial support groups now function on many university campuses around the country (e.g., New York University, Harvard, Yale, Kansas State, University of Michigan, Stanford, and the University of California [Brown, 1995]). In many communities, especially major metropolitan areas, support groups exist for interracial couples and their families. These support groups include informative newsletters, educational programs for parents, and social activities for the couples and their families (e.g., The Interracial Family Circle, P.O. Box 53290, Washington, D.C. 20009).

Support groups can also help answer a question that Alipuria (1990) asked, that of whether or not interracial people could develop a unique syncretic culture that can be passed on to the next generation. Alipuria felt that this new culture could provide role models and a reference group identity that could be vital in empowerment of interracial individuals.

Challenge 3

Work to Integrate Multicultural Aspects in All School Developmental Guidance Programs and in Community Settings

In writing the chapters on counselor roles with interracial children and adolescents, I became painfully aware of how little there is in the counseling literature on developmental multicultural counseling. The decision to integrate multicultural aspects into programs for all children and adolescents, not just interracial youth, was deliberate.

Many textbooks now include multicultural components. There are a wealth of materials on multicultural education and on developmental guidance that can be combined with textbook content to deliver positive programs. Suggestions in the *Teaching Tolerance* magazine address both the cognitive and affective aspects of the process of multicultural development. Counselor team work with teachers and parents is a critical component of these programs.

Community organizations provide other opportunities for counselors to get involved with educational programs that focus on broadening awareness of the needs of *all* people. The myths and stereotypes about interracial people presented and reiterated in this book can be addressed and challenged. Through presenting accurate and up-to-date information, the counselor plays a role in bringing about attitudinal change toward people of color and toward interracial people.

Challenge 4

Work to Broaden the Concept of Racial Identity to Include Identities Beyond That of One's Racial/Ethnic Heritage

In Wehrly (1995) I propose that "it is time to search for identity models that transcend identification with one's racial and ethnic heritage" (p. 226). A six-stage model for multiethnic education that included expanded ethnic identities was proposed more than a decade ago by Banks (1981). Positive identification with one's own racial heritage occurs at Stage 3. The fourth, fifth, and sixth stages include achieving positive identifications, and functioning in two ethnic environments (Stage 4), a national multiethnic citizenry (Stage 5), and a global/world ethnic community (Stage 6).

Hoare (1991) emphasized the importance of group identities for the survival of the species. She also underscored the fact that group identities can lead to feelings of superiority, exclusivity, and attempts to dominate (or even exterminate) people perceived to be different or of lesser status. Hoare (1991) called for mature identities that "extend beyond an individualistic self to a generative caring for other groups and for the entire human species" (p. 51).

With the rise in hate groups in the United States and abundant evidence of interethnic fighting in several areas of the world, counselors need to accept the challenge of supporting tolerance and preventing prejudice. These efforts assist individuals of any racial or ethnic heritage in building the positive levels of identification posited by Banks in Stages 4, 5, and 6.

Challenge 5

Expand Participation in Research Efforts to Develop and Test Counseling Theories to Improve Counseling Interventions With Interracial People

The knowledge base from interracial identity development research is lopsided and incomplete. Some biracial/interracial ethnic groups and developmental levels have received much attention while others have been given little or no attention.

Counselors are the people on the front line. Counselors are the individuals who can cooperate with researchers to move the profession forward on delivery of culturally sensitive services to the interracial population.

Parting Words

Summarizing this chapter would serve no useful purpose. Instead, I leave readers with this thought-provoking quote from the popular press:

> Changing our thinking about race will require a revolution in thought as profound, and profoundly unsettling, as anything science has ever demanded. What these researchers are talking about is changing the way in which we see the world—and each other. . . . We must ask science, also, why it is that we are so intent on sorting humanity into so few groups—us and Other—in the first place. (Begley, 1995, p. 69)

A

Proposed Cross-Cultural Competencies and Objectives

I. Counselor Awareness of Own Cultural Values and Biases
   A. Attitudes and Beliefs
      1. Culturally skilled counselors have moved from being culturally unaware to being aware and sensitive to their own cultural heritage and to valuing and respecting differences.
      2. Culturally skilled counselors are aware of how their own cultural backgrounds and experiences and attitudes, values, and biases influence psychological processes.

3. Culturally skilled counselors are able to recognize the limits of their competencies and expertise.

4. Culturally skilled counselors are comfortable with differences that exist between themselves and clients in terms of race, ethnicity, culture, and beliefs.

B. Knowledge

1. Culturally skilled counselors have specific knowledge about their own racial and cultural heritage and how it personally and professionally affects their definitions of normality-abnormality and the process of counseling.

2. Culturally skilled counselors possess knowledge and understanding about how oppression, racism, discrimination, and stereotyping affect them personally and in their work. This allows them to acknowledge their own racist attitudes, beliefs, and feelings. Although this standard applies to all groups, for White counselors it may mean that they understand how they may have directly or indirectly benefitted from individual, institutional, and cultural racism (White identity development models).

3. Culturally skilled counselors possess knowledge about their social impact on others. They are knowledgeable about communication style differences, how their style may clash or foster the counseling process with minority clients, and how to anticipate the impact it may have on others.

C. Skills

1. Culturally skilled counselors seek out educational, consultative, and training experience to improve their understanding and effectiveness in working with culturally different populations. Being able to recognize the limits of their competencies, they (a) seek consultation, (b) seek further training or education, (c) refer out to more qualified individuals or resources, or (d) engage in a combination of these.

2. Culturally skilled counselors are constantly seeking to understand themselves as racial and cultural beings and are actively seeking a nonracist identity.

II. Counselor Awareness of Client's Worldview
  A. Attitudes and Beliefs
    1. Culturally skilled counselors are aware of their negative emotional reactions toward other racial and ethnic groups that may prove detrimental to their clients in counseling. They are willing to contrast their own beliefs and attitudes with those of their culturally different clients in a nonjudgmental fashion.
    2. Culturally skilled counselors are aware of their stereotypes and preconceived notions that they may hold toward other racial and ethnic minority groups.
  B. Knowledge
    1. Culturally skilled counselors possess specific knowledge and information about the particular group they are working with. They are aware of the life experiences, cultural heritage, and historical background of their culturally different clients. This particular competency is strongly linked to the "minority identity development models" available in the literature.
    2. Culturally skilled counselors understand how race, culture, ethnicity, and so forth may affect personality formation, vocational choices, manifestation of psychological disorders, help-seeking behavior, and the appropriateness or inappropriateness of counseling approaches.
    3. Culturally skilled counselors understand and have knowlege about sociopolitical influences that impinge upon the life of racial and ethnic minorities. Immigration issues, poverty, racism, stereotyping, and powerlessness all leave major scars that may influence the counseling process.
  C. Skills
    1. Culturally skilled counselors should familiarize themselves with relevant research and the latest findings regarding mental health and mental disorders of various ethnic and racial groups. They should actively seek out educational experiences that foster their knowledge, understanding, and cross-cultural skills.

      2. Culturally skilled counselors become actively involved with minority individuals outside of the counseling setting (community events, social and political functions, celebrations, friendships, neighborhood groups, and so forth) so that their perspective of minorities is more than an academic or helping exercise.

III. Culturally Appropriate Intervention Strategies
   A. Attitudes and Beliefs
      1. Culturally skilled counselors respect clients' religious and/or spiritual beliefs and values, including attributions and taboos, because they affect worldview, psychosocial functioning, and expressions of distress.
      2. Culturally skilled counselors respect indigenous helping practices and respect minority community intrinsic help-giving networks.
      3. Culturally skilled counselors value bilingualism and do not view another language as an impediment to counseling (monolingualism may be the culprit).
   B. Knowledge
      1. Culturally skilled counselors have a clear and explicit knowledge and understanding of the generic characteristics of counseling and therapy (culture bound, class bound, and monolingual) and how they may clash with the cultural values of various minority groups.
      2. Culturally skilled counselors are aware of institutional barriers that prevent minorities from using mental health services.
      3. Culturally skilled counselors have knowledge of the potential bias in assessment instruments and use procedures and interpret findings keeping in mind the cultural and linguistic characteristics of the clients.
      4. Culturally skilled counselors have knowledge of the minority family structures, hierarchies, values, and beliefs. They are knowledgeable about the community characteristics and the resources in the community as well as the family.

5. Culturally skilled counselors are aware of relevant discriminatory practices at the social and community level that may be affecting the psychological welfare of the population being served.

C. Skills

1. Culturally skilled counselors are able to engage in a variety of verbal and nonverbal helping responses. They are able to *send* and *receive* both *verbal* and *nonverbal* messages *accurately* and *appropriately*. They are not tied down to only one method or approach to helping but recognize that helping styles and approaches may be culture bound. When they sense that their helping style is limited and potentially inappropriate, they can anticipate and ameliorate its negative impact.

2. Culturally skilled counselors are able to exercise institutional intervention skills on behalf of their clients. They can help clients determine whether a "problem" stems from racism or bias in others (the concept of health paranoia) so that clients do not inappropriately personalize problems.

3. Culturally skilled counselors are not averse to seeking consultation with traditional healers and religious and spiritual leaders and practitioners in the treatment of culturally different clients when appropriate.

4. Culturally skilled counselors take responsibility for interacting in the language requested by the client and, if not feasible, make appropriate referral. A serious problem arises when the linguistic skills of a counselor do not match the language of the client. This being the case, counselors should (a) seek a translator with cultural knowledge and appropriate professional background and (b) refer to a knowledgeable and competent bilingual counselor.

5. Culturally skilled counselors have training and expertise in the use of traditional assessment and testing instruments. They not only understand the technical aspects of the instruments but are also aware of the cultural

limitations. This allows them to use test instruments for the welfare of the diverse clients.

6. Culturally skilled counselors should attend to as well as work to eliminate biases, prejudices, and discriminatory practices. They should be cognizant of sociopolitical contexts in conducting evaluations and providing interventions and should develop sensitivity to issues of oppression, sexism, elitism, and racism.

7. Culturally skilled counselors take responsibility in educating their clients to the processes of psychological intervention, such as goals, expectations, legal rights, and the counselor's orientation.

Note. From "Multicultural Counseling Competencies and Standards: A Call to the Profession" by D. W. Sue, P. Arredondo, and R. J. McDavis, 1992, *Journal of Counseling and Development*, 70, pp. 484–486. Copyright 1992 by *Journal of Counseling and Development*. Reprinted by permission.

APPENDIX B

Interracial Books and Stories

Publication of children's books addressing interracial issues seems to have followed the societal trends of acceptance of interracial individuals. Most of the interracial books published before the mid-1970s addressed transracial or interracial adoption, particularly transracial adoption from other countries. In books published before 1989, little mention was made of interracial children in the United States whose parents had different heritages. More recent stories for children and adolescents address the issues of being biracial/interracial or of living in an interracial family. In addition, issues of interracial boy–girl relationships are appearing in stories and books. Narratives of interracial adoption continue to be the theme of many of the books, however.

In the list of stories and novels included in Appendix B, at least one of the lead characters is interracial, or the mother and father are of different racial heritages, or the family is interracial by virtue of a transracial adoption or foster placement. Books chosen for use with children and adolescents are selected from (a) annotations in the first five volumes of *The Bookfinder* (Dreyer, 1977, 1981, 1985, 1989, 1994) and in *Our Family, Our Friends, Our World—An Annotated Guide to Significant Multicultural Books for Children and Teenagers* (Miller-Lachmann, 1992); (b) books reviewed by Capan and Suarez (1993); and (c) the author's perusal of recent books and book listings.

The books in this suggested reading list are arranged by the suggested developmental age for which the book is written. Also noted are some of the psychological, behavioral, and developmental topics of the story. Readers may gain additional information on most of the books published through 1990 by referring to the extensive annotations for the book in the appropriate volume of *The Bookfinder* as listed here. (Note the year of publication of the book in order to locate the book in the appropriate volume of *The Bookfinder*):

Dreyer, S. S. (1977). *The Bookfinder: A Guide to Children's Literature About the Needs and Problems of Youth Aged 2–15.* Circle Pines, MN: American Guidance Service, Inc. (Includes annotations of 1,031 **books published before 1975**).

Dreyer, S. S. (1981). *The Bookfinder, Volume 2: A Guide to Children's Literature About the Needs and Problems of Youth Aged 2–15.* Circle Pines, MN: American Guidance Service. (Includes annotations of 723 **books published 1975 through 1978**).

Dreyer, S. S. (1985). *The Bookfinder: When Kids Need Books.* Circle Pines, MN: American Guidance Service. (Includes annotations of 725 **books published 1979 through 1982**).

Dreyer, S. S. (1989). *The Bookfinder 4: When Kids Need Books.* Circle Pines, MN: American Guidance Service. (Includes annotations of 731 **books published 1983 through 1986**).

Dreyer, S. S. (1994). *The Bookfinder, Volume 5: A Guide to Children's Literature about the Needs and Problems of Youth Aged 2–18.* Circle Pines, MN: American Guidance Service. (Includes annotations of 749 **books published 1987 through 1990**).

Miller-Lachmann's book, *Our Family, Our Friends, Our World* (1992), includes annotations as well as a critique of each of 1,038 books published between 1970 and 1990. Listings in this annotated guide are by 18 regions of the world and by grade levels (Preschool–3, 4–6, 7–9, and 10–12.

INTERRACIAL BOOKS AND STORIES

Ages 3–5:

Mower, N. A. (1984). *I visit my tutu and grandma*. Kailua, HI: Press Pacifica. (Interracial Hawaiian-Caucasian girl tells of activities she shares with her paternal Hawaiian grandmother and her maternal Caucasian grandmother).

Ages 3–8:

Davol, M. W. (1993). *Black, white, just right!*. Niles, IL: Albert Whitman & Co. (An upbeat, rhyming story of how a biracial child celebrates the differences in her family).

Elliott, O. (1989). *Under Sammy's bed*. New York: Puffin. (Interracial family with Black mother and White father helps Sammy, a preschooler and the youngest child, overcome fears).

Hale, S. J. (1990). *Mary had a little lamb*. New York: Scholastic. (Adaptation of the well-known nursery rhyme to contemporary time with a biracial African American-White girl as the lead character).

Mandelbaum, P. (1993). *You be me: I'll be you*. Brooklyn, New York: Kane/Miller Book Publishers. (Interracial child feeling discrimination because she looks different. Father helps the child accept her unique heritage). Published first in Belgium.

Turner, A. (1990). *Through moon and stars and the night skies*. New York: HarperCollins. (Interracial adoption of a child from an orphanage in Asia; fear of the unknown).

Ages 4–6:

Ahlberg, J., & Ahlberg, A. (1988). *Starting school*. New York: Viking Kestrel. (Picture-book format of everyday events for children starting first grade; includes child from an interracial family).

Ages 4–8:

Adoff, A. (1973). *Black is brown is tan*. New York: Harper & Row. (Poem-story about an interracial family).

Bunin, C., & Bunin, S. (1976). *Is that your sister? A true story of adoption.* New York: Pantheon Books. (Interracial adoption following foster home placement; describes the adoption process and feelings of an adopted child).

Milgram, M. (1978). *Brothers are all the same.* New York: E. P. Dutton & Co. (Interracial adoption).

Williams, V. B. (1990). *More more more said the baby.* New York: Green-willow. (In the second of three stories, an African American child and his White grandmother are interacting).

Ages 4–9:

Gabel, S. (1989). *Where the sun kisses the sea.* Indianapolis, IN: Perspectives Press. (Interracial adoption; Asian American orphan; living in children's home; accepting change).

Ages 5–9:

Girard, L. W. (1989). *We adopted you, Benjamin Koo.* Niles, IL: Albert Whitman & Co. (Interracial adoption; Korean American; search for identity; struggles to accept the situation).

Spohn, D. (1991). *Winter wood.* New York: Lothrop, Lee & Shepard. (Father and son share work in an interracial family).

Ages 6–8:

Adoff, A. (1991). *Hard to be six.* New York: Lothrop, Lee & Shepard. (A six-year-old in an interracial, interfaith family describes how hard it is to be six).

Friedman, I. R. (1984). *How my parents learned to eat.* Boston: Houghton Mifflin. (Interracial marriage; Japanese American; biracial).

Ages 7–10:

Angel, A. (1988). *Real for sure sister.* Indianapolis, IN: Perspectives Press. (Interracial adoption of 4 children [one biracial]; ethnic/racial prejudice).

Heath, A. (1992). *Sofie's role.* New York: Four Winds Press. (Biracial child helps out in her parents' bakery at Christmas).

Rosenberg, M. B. (1986). *Living in two worlds.* New York: Lothrop, Lee & Shepard. (Photoessay of several interracial families. Challenges and benefits from interracial family life).

Welber, R. (1972). *The train.* New York: Pantheon. (Interracial family, African American-Asian and their 4 children; overcoming fear).

Ages 7–11:

Sobol, H. L. (1984). *We don't look like our mom and dad*. New York: Coward-McCann. (Photoessay of the interracial adoption of two Korean boys).

Ages 8–11:

Banks, S. H. (1993). *Remember my name*. New York: Rinehart. (Historical story of biracial child [half-Indian, half Scottish] who goes to live with her uncle in Georgia in the 1830s).

McDonald, J. (1988). *Mail-order kid*. New York: Putnam & Grosset Group. (Interracial adoption; Korean American).

Ages 8–12:

Buck, P. S. (1966). *Matthew, Mark, Luke, and John*. New York: John Day. (Interracial adoption; biracial Korean American orphan).

Rosenberg, M. (1984). *Being adopted*. New York: Lothrop, Lee & Shepard. (Story of three children adopted by families of different racial and cultural roots).

Ages 9–11:

McHugh, B. E. (1983). *Karen's sister*. New York: Greenwillow Books. (Interracial adoption).

McHugh, B. E. (1983). *Raising a mother isn't easy*. New York: Greenwillow Books. (Interracial adoption).

Ages 9–12:

Miles, B. (1976). *All it takes is practice*. New York: Alfred A. Knopf. (Interracial marriage; ethnic-racial prejudice).

Ages 9 and up:

Hopkins, L. B. (1992). *Through our eyes: Poems and pictures about growing up*. Boston: Little, Brown. (Photographs and poems celebrate 16 culturally diverse children. The poem and photograph of "Lisa," a biracial child, ask the reader to view her as a unique individual).

Hoyt-Goldsmith, D. (1990). *Totem pole*. New York: Holiday House. (Biracial son of a Native American father and a Caucasian mother talks about how his father carves totem poles and the traditions and history of the Eagle Clan of the Tsimshian tribe in the state of Washington).

Krementz, J. (1982). *How it feels to be adopted*. New York: Alfred A. Knopf. (Reports from 19 children who have been interracially adopted).

Paterson, K. (1988). *Park's quest*. New York: Dutton. (Interracial family, Vietamese American, and an 11-year-old's search for family and inner peace).

Rosenberg, M. B. (1989). *Growing up adopted*. New York: Bradbury Press. (Interracial adoption; search for identity).

Ages 10–13:

Nichols, J. K. (1985). *All but the right folks*. Owings Mills, MD: Stemmer House Publishers. (A biracial Black-White child's search for identity).

Sachs, M. (1973). *The truth about Mary Rose*. New York: Doubleday. (Biracial child's search to learn more about her aunt).

Ure, J. (1985). *The most important thing*. New York: William Morrow & Co. (Boy-girl relationships: interracial).

Ages 10 and up:

Klein, N. (1975). *What it's all about*. New York: Dial Publishers. (Troubles of an 11-year-old biracial girl [Japanese American father and White mother] whose parents divorce).

Neufeld, J. (1968). *Edgar Allan*. New York: Signet. (Interracial adoption of a Black child by a White family; pains of ethnic/racial prejudice in a small all-White town).

Ages 11–14:

Danziger, P. (1982). *The divorce express*. New York: Delacorte Press. (Biracial best friend of 14-year-old girl whose parents are divorced and have joint custody of her).

Danziger, P. (1985). *It's an aardvark-eat-turtle world*. New York: Delacorte Press. (Biracial—sequel to *Divorce Express*).

Ages 11 and up:

Adoff, A. (1982). *All the colors of the race*. New York: Lothrop. (Poems expressing the feelings of an interracial African American-White child).

Terris, S. (1974). *Whirling rainbows*. New York: Doubleday. (Interracial adoption; search for identity).

Wyeth, S. D. (1994). *The world of daughter*. New York: Delacorte Press. (Story of an interracial eleven-year-old of Italian, African American, Irish Catholic, and Jewish heritage; the discrimination she experiences; and the excitement she feels in exploring her family heritage as a school project).

Ages 12 and up:

Gay, K. (1987). *The rainbow effect: Interracial families*. New York: Franklin Watts. (Informational book on issues faced by teenagers growing up in an interracial family; appreciating racial differences as well as commonalities).

Hamilton, V. (1976). *Arilla sun down*. New York: Greenwillow. (Interracial family; Native American-African American; complexities of family heritage identity search).

Hamilton, V. (1993). *Plain city*. New York: Blue Sky. (Story of a 12-year-old racially mixed girl's search for harmony and identity).

Irwin, H. (1987). *Kim/Kimi*. New York: Margaret K. McElderry Books. (Biracial; Japanese Caucasian; search for identity).

Meyer, C. (1990). *Denny's Tapes*. New York: Margaret K. McElderry Books. (Interracial marriage; search for identity; interracial adolescent relationships).

Okimoto, J. D. (1990). *Molly by any other name*. New York: Scholastic. (Interracial adoption; search for family heritage and identity).

Ruckman, I. (1983). *The Hunger Scream*. New York: Walker and Co. (Interracial adolescent relationships).

Voight, C. (1985). *The runner*. New York: Atheneum. (Biracial adult befriends a 14-year-old psychologically abused male).

Ages 13 and up:

Bellingham, B. (1983). *Storm child*. New York: Dell. (Historical fiction of a Scottish Factor [manager of a trading post] in western Canada who takes a Native Canadian wife. When their biracial daughter, Storm Child, is 13 her father deserts the family and returns to Scotland. The story narrates the struggles of Storm Child to establish a biracial identity and is representative of the Metis or Burnt Wood people of the Canadian West who were the children of the European-Native Canadian marriages).

Bunting, A. E. (1985). *Face at the edge of the world*. Boston: Houghton Mifflin. (Interracial adolescent relationships).

Dorris, M. (1987). *A yellow raft in blue water*. New York: Henry Holt. (Story of three generations of Native American women and their intertwined lives; first story focuses on a 15-year-old girl whose father is African American and mother is Native American).

Garland, S. (1992). *Song of the buffalo boy*. San Diego, CA: Harcourt Brace Jovanovich. (17-year-old Vietnamese American teenager faces treatment as an outcast in Vietnam and a decision as to whether to apply to come to the United States under the Amerasian Homecoming Act).

Guernsey, J. A. B. (1986). *Room to breathe*. New York: Clarion Books. (Interracial adolescent relationships; ethnic/racial prejudice).

Katz, W. L., & Franklin, P. A. (1993). *Proudly red and black: Stories of African and Native Americans*. New York: Atheneum. (Brief biographies of six biracial Native American-African American people who have played important roles in the early history of our nation).

Lipsyte, R. (1991). *The Brave*. New York: HarperCollins. (Story of a biracial young man's quest for identity and inner peace; Native American-White).

Markle, S. (1992). *The fledglings*. New York: Bantam. (14-year-old interracial orphan girl's quest for her Cherokee Indian paternal grandfather and their development of a trusting relationship).

Paulsen, G. (1991). *The monument*. New York: Delacorte. (Story of an adopted mixed-race 13-year-old girl in a rural Kansas farming community).

Porte, B. A. (1987). *I only made up the roses*. New York: Greenwillow. (17-year-old White girl's family becomes interracial through the remarriage of her mother; biracial brother; family nurturing; development of family pride).

Ages 14 and up:

Bode, J. (1989). *Different worlds: Interracial and cross-cultural dating*. New York: Franklin Watts. (Handbook for teenagers in relationships with people of other races or cultures. Information from interviews with teenage couples, parents, educators, and health professionals).

Butler, O. E. (1979). *Kindred*. Boston: Beacon. (Fictional account that incorporates historical background of interracial relationships).

Jones, T. (1986). *Skindeep*. New York: Harper & Row. (Biracial; apartheid, South Africa; ethnic/racial prejudice).

Rinaldi, A. (1991). *Wolf by the ears*. New York: Scholastic. (Historical account of one of the interracial daughters of Thomas Jefferson and his mulatto mistress).

Robinson, M. A. (1990). *A woman of her tribe*. New York: Scribner's Young Readers. (Interracial 15-year-old female's family life in two cultures, English mother and Nootika Indian grandmother, on Vancouver Island, Canada).

Roy, J. (1992). *Soul daddy*. San Diego, CA: Gulliver/Harcourt Brace Jovanovich. (Biracial 15-year-old twin daughters of a White mother and African American father adjust to life after their father returns from a long absence).

Sanders, D. (1990). *Clover*. Chapel Hill, NC: Algonquin Books of Chapel Hill. (Interracial marriage followed immediately by death of the African American father; White stepmother assumes the responsibility for raising her African American step-daughter; working through ethnic/racial prejudice).

Savage, D. (1992). *A stranger calls me home*. Boston: Houghton Mifflin. (16-year-old male returns to New Zealand and becomes friends with a half White and half Maori young man raised in a White home; the young men embark on a search to find the biracial youth's Maori father).

Sung, B. L. (1990). *Chinese American intermarriage*. New York: Center for Migration Studies. (Nonfiction report includes statistical and research information as well as anecdotal accounts from 50 Chinese couples in interracial marriages).

Adult:

Bates, J. D. (1993). *Gift children: A story of race, family, and adoption in a divided America*. New York: Ticknor & Fields. (Biographical account of the challenges of cross-racial adoption of an African American daughter and a biracial African American-White daughter by a White couple with two sons. The story covers 23 years of interracial life by the Bates family. It includes first-person accounts from the four children and other family relatives and addresses the complexities of dealing with both covert and overt racism.)

Funderburg, L. (1994). *Black, White, other: Biracial Americans talk about race and identity*. New York: William Morrow. (In-depth oral histories from interviews with 46 biracial adult children with one Black and one White parent. These biracial individuals present their candid stories and opinions on growing up and living in contemporary United States.)

Graham, L. O. (1995). *Member of the club: Reflections on life in a racially polarized world*. New York: HarperCollins. (Chapter 2, "I Never Dated a White Girl: Why Some Blacks Still Oppose Interracial Marriage," gives reasons some White people disapprove of interracial marriage and discusses six objections that some Black people have to interracial coupling.)

Haizlip, S. T. (1994). *The sweeter the juice: A family memoir in Black and White*. New York: Simon & Schuster. (The autobiographical account of

REFERENCES

Aboud, F. E. (1987). The development of ethnic self-identification and attitudes. In J. S. Phinney & M. J. Rotheram (Eds.), *Children's ethnic socialization: Pluralism and development* (pp. 32–55). Newbury Park, CA: Sage.

Adler, A. (1987). Children and biracial identity. In A. Thomas & J. Grimes (Eds.), *Children's needs: Psychological perspectives* (pp. 56–61). Washington, DC: National Association of School Psychologists.

Alipuria, L. L. (1990). *Self esteem and self label in multiethnic students from two southern California state universities.* Unpublished master's thesis. California State University, Los Angeles, CA.

Allport, G. W. (1954). *The nature of prejudice.* Reading, MA: Addison-Wesley.

Anaya, R. (1973). *Bless me Ultima.* Berkeley, CA: Quinto Sol Publications.

Anderson, K. S. (1993). Ethnic identity in biracial Asian Americans. *Dissertation Abstracts International, 54/09–B,* 4905.

Angelou, M. (1970). *I know why the caged bird sings.* New York: Random House.

Aronson, D. (1995, Spring). Heroic possibilities. *Teaching Tolerance,* pp. 11–15.

Aten, J. (1982). *Americans, too! Understanding American minorities through research-related activities.* Carthage, IL: Good Apple.

Atkinson, D. R., & Hackett, G. (1995). *Counseling diverse populations.* Dubuque, IA: Brown & Benchmark.

Atkinson, D. R., Morten, G., & Sue, D. W. (1979). *Counseling American minorities: A cross cultural perspective.* Dubuque, IA: W. C. Brown.

Atkinson, D. R., Morten, G., & Sue, D. W. (1983). *Counseling American minorities: A cross cultural perspective* (2nd ed.). Dubuque, IA: W. C. Brown.

Atkinson, D. R., Morten, G., & Sue, D. W. (1989). *Counseling American minorities: A cross cultural perspective* (3rd ed.). Dubuque, IA: W. C. Brown.

Atkinson, D. R., Morten, G., & Sue, D. W. (1993). *Counseling American minorities: A cross-cultural perspective* (4th ed.). Dubuque, IA: Brown & Benchmark.

Aubrey, R. (1995, February 19). A white boy who learned he was black crossed color line anyway. *The San Diego Union-Tribune*, p. A-35.

Axelson, J. A. (1993). *Counseling and development in a multicultural society* (2nd ed.). Pacific Grove, CA: Brooks/Cole.

Banks, J. A. (1981). *Multiethnic education: Theory and practice*. Boston: Allyn & Bacon.

Baptiste, D. A. (1984). Marital and family therapy with racially/culturally intermarried stepfamilies: Issues and guidelines. *Family Relations, 33*, 373–380.

Baptiste, D. A. (1990). Therapeutic strategies with Black/Hispanic families: Identity problems of a neglected minority. *Journal of Family Psychotherapy, 1*(3), 15–38.

Baruth, L. G., & Manning, M. L. (1991). *Multicultural counseling and psychotherapy: A lifespan perspective*. New York: Merrill.

Bates, J. D. (1993). *Gift children: A story of race, family, and adoption in a divided America*. New York: Ticknor & Fields.

Begley, S. (1995, February 13). Three is not enough. *Newsweek*, pp. 67–69.

Bennett, L. A. (Ed.). (1992). *Encyclopedia of world cultures: Europe, (Vol. 4), (central, western, and southeastern Europe)*. Boston: G. K. Hall.

Bowles, D. D. (1993). Bi-racial identity: Children born to African-American and White couples. *Clinical Social Work Journal, 21*, 417–428.

Brandell, J. R. (1988). Treatment of the biracial child: Theoretical and clinical issues. *Journal of Multicultural Counseling and Development, 16*, 176–187.

Brody, H. (1984). Growing up in interracial families: Suggestions for single parents. *Interracial Books for Children BULLETIN, 15*(6), 12–13.

Brown, J. A. (1987). Casework contacts with black-white couples. *Social Casework, 68*, 24–29.

Brown, U. M. (1991). A study of racial identity, conflict, self-esteem and experiential/physical factors in young adults with one black and one white parent. *Dissertation Abstracts, 53/06A*, 2116.

Brown, U. M. (1995). Black/White interracial young adults: Quest for a racial identity. *American Journal of Orthopsychiatry, 65*, 125–130.

Burrell, C. (1995, April 14). Foundation battles 'last Jim Crow law.' *St. Louis Post-Dispatch*, p. 5B.

Camarata, C. (1991). Making connections: Introducing multicultural books. *School Library Journal, 37,* 190–191.

Capan, M. A. (1994). Exploring biracial/biethnic characters in young adult and children's books. *MultiCultural Review, 3*(4), 14–19.

Capan, M. A., & Suarez, C. (1993). Biracial/biethnic characters in young adult and children's books. *MultiCultural Review, 2*(2), 32–37.

Carnes, J. (1995). *Us and them: A history of intolerance in America.* Montgomery, AL: Southern Poverty Law Center.

Chavira, V., & Phinney, J. S. (1991). Adolescents' ethnic identity, self-esteem, and strategies for dealing with ethnicity and minority status. *Hispanic Journal of Behavioral Sciences, 13,* 226–227.

Chen, C. L. (1984). Growing up in interracial families: Growing up with an Asian American heritage. *Interracial Books for Children BULLETIN, 15*(6), 11–12.

Comer, J. P. (1988). Establishing a positive racial identity, *Parents, 63,* 167.

Cornett, C. E., & Cornett, C. F. (1980). *Bibliotherapy: The right book at the right time.* Bloomington, IN: Phi Delta Kappa.

Cose, E. (1995, February 13). One drop of bloody history. *Newsweek*, pp. 70, 72.

Cottrell, A. B. (1990). Cross-national marriages: A review of the literature. *Journal of Comparative Family Studies, 21,* 151–169.

Courtney, B. A. (1995, February 13). Freedom from choice: Being biracial has meant denying half of my identity, *Newsweek*, p. 16.

Cross, W. E. (1971). The Negro-to-Black conversion experience: Toward a psychology of Black liberation. *Black World, 20,* 13–17.

Cross, W. E., Jr. (1991). *Shades of Black: Diversity in African-American identity.* Philadelphia: Temple University Press.

Crumbley, J., Aarons, J., & Fraser, W. E. (1995). Options to anger: Skills for reducing violence among adolescents. *Counseling and Human Development, 27*(6), 1–8.

Davidson, J. R. (1992). Theories about Black-White interracial marriage: A clinical perspective. *Journal of Multicultural Counseling and Development, 20,* 150–157.

Davis, F. J. (1991). *Who is Black? One nation's definition.* University Park, PA: Pennsylvania State University Press.

Delany, S. L., Delany, A. E., & Hearth, A. H. (1993). *Having our say.* New York: Bantam Doubleday Dell.

Dreyer, S. S. (1977). *The bookfinder.* Circle Pines, MN: American Guidance Services.

Dreyer, S. S. (1981). *The bookfinder* (Volume 2). Circle Pines, MN: American Guidance Services.

Dreyer, S. S. (1985). *The bookfinder 3: When kids need books.* Circle Pines, MN: American Guidance Services.

Dreyer, S. S. (1989). *The bookfinder 4: When kids need books.* Circle Pines, MN: American Guidance Services.

Dreyer, S. S. (1994). *The bookfinder* (Volume 5). Circle Pines, MN: American Guidance Services.

Erikson, E. H. (1950). *Childhood and society.* New York: Norton.

Erikson, E. H. (1963). *Childhood and society* (2nd ed.). New York: Norton.

Erikson, E. H. (1968). *Identity: Youth and crisis.* New York: Norton.

Erikson, E. H. (1980). *Identity and the life cycle.* New York: Norton.

Evans, M. M. (1993, November 8). Transracial adoption: Questions and challenges for children & parents alike. *The Washington Post*, p. B5.

Exum, H. A. (1983). Key issues in family counseling with gifted and talented black students. *Roeper Review , 5*(3), 28–31.

Faulkner, J., & Kich, G. K. (1983). Assessment and engagement stages in therapy with the interracial family. In J. C. Hansen & C. J. Falicov (Eds.), *Cultural perspectives in family therapy* (pp. 78–90). Rockville, MD: Aspen.

Folaron, G., & Hess, P. M. (1993). Placement considerations for children of mixed African American and Caucasian parentage. *Child Welfare, 72,* 113–125.

Funderburg, L. (1994). *Black, white, other: Biracial Americans talk about race and identity.* New York: William Morrow.

Gay, K. (1987). *The rainbow effect: Interracial families.* New York: Franklin Watts.

Gibbs, J. T. (1985). Treatment relationships with Black clients: Interpersonal vs. instrumental strategies. In C. B. Germain, P. Caroff, P. L. Ewalt, P. Glasser, and R. Vaughan (Eds.), *Advances in clinical social work practice* (pp. 184–195). Silver Spring, MD: National Association of Social Workers.

Gibbs, J. T. (1987). Identity and marginality: Issues in the treatment of biracial adolescents. *American Journal of Orthopsychiatry, 57,* 265–278.

Gibbs, J. T. (1989). Biracial adolescents. In J. T. Gibbs, L. N. Huang, & Associates (Eds.), *Children of color: Psychological interventions with minority youth* (pp. 322–350). San Francisco: Jossey-Bass.

Gibbs, J. T., & Hines, A. M. (1992). Negotiating ethnic identity: Issues for Black-White biracial adolescents. In M. P. P. Root (Ed.), *Racially mixed people in America* (pp. 223–238). Newbury Park, CA: Sage.

Goodman, M. E. (1952). *Race awareness in young children*. Cambridge, MA: Addison-Wesley Press.

Gonzalez, K. (1995, Spring). Family I-Search, *Teaching Tolerance*, p. 8.

Graham, L. O. (1995). *Member of the club: Reflections of life in a racially polarized world*. New York: HarperCollins.

Griswold, V. J., & Starke, J. (1987). *Multi-Cultural Art Projects*. Denver: Love Publishing.

Gunthorpe, W. W. (1977). Skin color recognition, preference and identification in interracial children: A comparative study. *Dissertation Abstracts International, 38*(7B), 3468–3469.

Haizlip, S. T. (1994). *The sweeter the juice*. New York: Simon & Schuster.

Haizlip, S. T. (1995, February/March). Passing. *American Heritage*, pp. 46–53.

Hall, C. C. I. (1980). The ethnic identity of racially mixed people: A study of Black-Japanese. *Dissertation Abstracts International, 41*(4-B), 1565-1566.

Hall, C. C. I. (1992). Please choose one: Ethnic identity choices for biracial individuals. In M. P. P. Root (Ed.), *Racially mixed people in America* (pp. 250–264). Newbury Park, CA: Sage.

Hatcher, C. L. (1987). *"It's only half of me." The interracial child: The need for balance*. (ERIC Document Reproduction Service No. ED 336 970).

Havemann, J. (1995, April 25). HHS eases barriers to interracial adoptions. *The Washington Post*, p. A10.

Helbig, A. K., & Perkins, A. R. (1994). *This land is our land—A guide to multicultural literature for children and young adults*. Westport, CT: Greenwood Press.

Helms, J. E. (1984). Toward a theoretical explanation of the effects of race on counseling: A Black and White model. *The Counseling Psychologist, 12*, 153–165.

Helms, J. E. (1985). Cultural identity in the treatment process. In P. Pedersen (Ed.), *Handbook of Cross-Cultural Counseling and Therapy* (pp. 239–245). Westport, CT: Greenwood Press.

Helms, J. E. (Ed.). (1990). *Black and white racial identity: Theory, research, and practice*. New York: Greenwood Press.

Helms, J. E. (1992). *A race is a nice thing to have*. Topeka, KS: Content Communications.

Henderson, P. (1990). Black and white protagonists in contemporary fiction: Findings and recommendations for interventions on race relations. *Journal of Multicultural Counseling and Development, 18,* 180–193.

Herbert, F. (1984). *Soul catcher.* New York: Avenel Books.

Herlihy, B., & Corey, G. (1992). *Dual relationships in counseling.* Alexandria, VA: American Counseling Association.

Herring, R. D. (1992). Biracial children: An increasing concern for elementary and middle school counselors. *Elementary School Guidance and Counseling, 27,* 123–130.

Herring, R. D. (1995). Developing biracial ethnic identity: A review of the increasing dilemma. *Journal of Multicultural Counseling and Development, 23,* 29–38.

Hill, M., & Peltzer, J. (1982). A report of thirteen groups for white parents of black children. *Family Relations, 31,* 557–565.

Hoare, C. H. (1991). Psychosocial identity development and cultural others. *Journal of Counseling and Development, 70,* 45–53.

Hockings, P. (Ed.). (1993). *Encyclopedia of world cultures: Vol. 5, East and southeast Asia.* Boston: G. K. Hall.

Holmes, S. A. (1995, April 13). Bitter racial dispute rages over adoption. *The New York Times,* p. A16.

Horning, K. T. (1993). The contributions of alternative press publishers to multicultural literature for children. *Library Trends, 41,* 524–540.

Hutchinson, R. L. (1990). Everybody has to be somewhere! *Journal of Mental Health Counseling, 12,* 96–98.

Ibrahim, F. A., & Schroeder, D. G. (1990). Cross-cultural couples counseling: A developmental, psychoeducational intervention. *Journal of Comparative Family Studies, 21,* 193–205.

"Interracial Dating: Yes or No?" (1993, March/April). Feedback. *The Black Collegian,* pp. 31–34.

Jacobs, J. H. (1977). Black/white interracial families: Marital process and identity development in young children. *Dissertation Abstracts International, 38*(10-B), 5023.

Jacobs, J. H. (1992) Identity development in biracial children. In M. P. P. Root (Ed.), *Racially mixed people in America* (pp. 190–206). Newbury Park, CA: Sage.

Johnson, D. J. (1992a). Developmental pathways: Toward an ecological theoretical formulation of race identity in Black-White biracial children. In M. P. P. Root (Ed.), *Racially mixed people in America* (pp. 37–49). Newbury Park, CA: Sage.

Johnson, D. J. (1992b). Racial preference and biculturality in biracial preschoolers. *Merrill-Palmer Quarterly, 38,* 233–244.

Johnson, L., & Smith, S. (1993). *Dealing with diversity through multicultural fiction—Library-classroom partnerships.* Chicago: American Library Association.

Johnson, R. C., & Nagoshi, C. T. (1986). The adjustment of offspring of within-group and interracial/intercultural marriages: A comparison of personality factor scores. *Journal of Marriage and the Family, 48,* 279–284.

Kahn, D. A. (1993). Transcultural family counseling: Theories and techniques. In J. McFadden (Ed.), *Transcultural counseling: Bilateral and international perspectives* (pp. 109–131). Alexandria, VA: American Counseling Association.

Kalmijn, M. (1993). Trends in black/white intermarriage. *Social Forces, 72,* 119–146.

Katz, P. A. (1987). Developmental and social processes in ethnic attitudes and self-identification. In J. S. Phinney & M. J. Rotheram (Eds.), *Children's ethnic socialization: Pluralism and development* (pp. 92–99). Newbury Park, CA: Sage.

Kerf-Wellington, J. (1992). *Black, white, or "other"? The development of a biracial identity.* Unpublished master's thesis, Loyola University of Chicago, Chicago, IL.

Kerwin, C. (1991). Racial identity development in biracial children of Black/White racial heritage. *Dissertation Abstracts International, 52/07-A,* 2469.

Kerwin, C., & Ponterotto, J. G. (1995). Biracial identity development: Theory and research. In J. G. Ponterotto, J. M. Casas, L. A. Suzuki, & C. M. Alexander (Eds.), *Handbook of multicultural counseling* (pp. 199–217). Thousand Oaks, CA: Sage.

Kerwin, C., Ponterotto, J. G., Jackson, B. L., & Harris, A. (1993). Racial identity in biracial children: A qualitative investigation. *Journal of Counseling Psychology, 40,* 221–231.

Kich, G. K. (1982). Eurasians: Ethnic/racial identity development of biracial Japanese/White adults. *Dissertation Abstracts International, 43*(10B), 3365.

Kich, G. K. (1992). The developmental process of asserting a biracial, bicultural identity. In M. P. P. Root (Ed.), *Racially mixed people in America* (pp. 304–317). Newbury Park, CA: Sage.

Kim, J. (1981). *Processes of Asian-American identity development: A study of*

Japanese American women's perceptions of their struggle to achieve positive identities as Americans of Asian ancestry. Unpublished doctoral dissertation, University of Massachusetts, Amherst.

Kleinman, A. (1985, February). *Culture in the clinic*. Paper presented at Third Annual Teachers College Roundtable for Cross-Cultural Counseling, Teachers College, Columbia University, New York City.

Kruse, G. M. (1992). No single season: Multicultural literature for all children. *Wilson Library Bulletin, 66*(6), 30–33, 122.

Lee, C. C. (Ed.). (1995). *Counseling for diversity: A guide for school counselors and related professionals*. Boston: Allyn & Bacon.

Lee, C. C., & Richardson, B. L. (Eds.). (1991). *Multicultural issues in counseling: New approaches to diversity*. Alexandria, VA: American Association of Counseling and Development.

Leslie, C., Elam, R., Samuels, A., & Senna, D. (1995, February 13). The loving generation. Biracial children seek their own place. *Newsweek*, p. 72.

Lipson, G. B., & Romatowski, J. A. (1983). *Ethnic pride: Explorations into your ethnic heritage: Cultural information—activities—student research*. Carthage, IL: Good Apple.

Locke, D. C. (1992). *Increasing multicultural understanding: A comprehensive model*. Newbury Park, CA: Sage.

Logan, S. L., Freeman, E. M., & McRoy, R. G. (1987). Racial identity problems of bi-racial clients: Implications for social work practice. *The Journal of Intergroup Relations, 15,* 11–24.

Lyles, M. R., Yancey, A., Grace, C., & Carter, J. H. (1985). Racial identity and self-esteem: Problems peculiar to biracial children. *Journal of the American Academy of Child Psychiatry, 24,* 150–153.

Mar, J. (1988). Chinese Caucasian interracial parenting and ethnic identity. *Dissertation Abstracts, 49/05A,* 1278A.

Marcia, J. E. (1966). Development and validation of ego-identity status. *Journal of Personality and Social Psychology, 3,* 551–558.

Marcia, J. E. (1980). Identity in adolescence. In J. Adelson (Ed.), *Handbook of adolescent psychology* (pp. 159–187). New York: John Wiley.

Marcus, E. (1992, March 8). In America, Amerasian odyssey: Few find the fathers who left them behind in Vietnam. *The Washington Post*, pp. A1, A16.

Mathabane, M., & Mathabane, G. (1992). *Love in black and white: The triumph of love over prejudice and taboo*. New York: HarperCollins.

McCormick, T. E. (1990). Counselor-teacher interface: Promoting nonsexist education and career development. *Journal of Multicultural Counseling and Development, 18,* 2–10.

McRoy, R. G., & Freeman E. (1986). Racial-identity issues among mixed-race children. *Social Work in Education, 8,* 164–175.

McRoy, R. G., & Zurcher, L. A., Jr. (1983). *Transracial and inracial adoptees: The adolescent years.* Springfield, IL: Charles C Thomas.

Melina, L. R. (1990, May). Racial identity of children of mixed heritage still controversial. *Adopted Child,* pp. 1–3.

Miller, R. L. (1992). The human ecology of multiracial identity. In M. P. P. Root (Ed.), *Racially mixed people in America* (pp. 24–36). Newbury Park, CA: Sage.

Miller, R. L., & Miller, B. (1990). Mothering the biracial child: Bridging the gaps between African-American and White parenting styles. *Women & Therapy, 10,* 169–180.

Miller-Lachmann, L. (1992). *Our family, our friends, our world—An annotated guide to significant multicultural books for children and teenagers.* New Providence, NJ: R. R. Bowker.

Morganthau, T. (1995, February 13). What color is black? *Newsweek,* pp. 62–65.

Mura, D. (1992, Sept/Oct). What should I tell Samantha, my biracial daughter, about secrets and anger? How is she going to choose an identity? *Mother Jones,* pp. 18–19, 21–22.

Murphy-Shigematsu, S. L. H. (1987). The voices of Amerasians: Ethnicity, identity, and empowerment in interracial Japanese Americans. *Dissertation Abstracts International, 48*(4B), 1143.

Myer, R., & James, R. K. (1989). Counseling internationally adopted children: A personal intervention approach. *Elementary School Guidance and Counseling, 23,* 324–328.

Nichols, J. K. (1985). *All but the right folks.* Owings Mills, MD: Stemmer House Publishers.

Nishimura, N. J. (1995). Addressing the needs of biracial children: An issue for counselors in a multicultural school environment. *The School Counselor, 43,* 52–57.

Omizo, M. M., & D'Andrea, M. J. (1995). Multicultural classroom guidance. In C. C. Lee (Ed.), *Counseling for diversity: A guide for school counselors and related professionals* (pp. 143–158). Boston: Allyn & Bacon.

Overmier, K. (1990). Biracial adolescents: Areas of conflict in identity formation. *The Journal of Applied Social Sciences, 14,* 157–176.

Parham, T. A., & Helms, J. E. (1981). The influence of black students' racial identity attitudes on preferences for counselor's race. *Journal of Counseling Psychology, 28,* 250–257.

Payne, R. B. (1977). Racial attitude formation in children of mixed black and white heritage: Skin color and racial identity. *Dissertation Abstracts International, 38*(6-B), 2876.

Pedersen, P. (1994). *A handbook for developing multicultural awareness* (2nd ed.). Alexandria, VA: American Counseling Association.

Pedersen, P. B., Draguns, J. G., Lonner, W. J., & Trimble, J. E. (Eds.). (1989). *Counseling across cultures* (3rd ed.). Honolulu: University of Hawaii Press.

Perkins, M. (1994, March 7). Guess who's coming to church? *Christianity Today,* pp. 30–33.

Phinney, J. S. (1989). Stages of ethnic identity development in minority group adolescents. *Journal of Early Adolescence, 9,* 34–49.

Phinney, J. S. (1992). The multigroup ethnic identity measure: A new scale for use with diverse groups. *Journal of Adolescent Research, 7,* 156–176.

Phinney, J. S. (1993). A three-stage model of ethnic identity in adolescence. In M. E. Bernal & G. P. Knight (Eds.), *Ethnic identity: Formation and transmission among Hispanics and other minorities* (pp. 61–79). Albany, NY: SUNY Press.

Phinney, J. S., & Alipuria, L. L. (1990). Ethnic identity in college students from four ethnic groups. *Journal of Adolescence, 13,* 171–183.

Phinney, J. S., & Chavira, V. (1992). Ethnic identity and self-esteem: An exploratory longitudinal study. *Journal of Adolescence, 15,* 272–281.

Phinney, J. S., Lochner, B. T., & Murphy, R. (1990). Ethnic identity development and psychological adjustment in adolescence. In A. R. Stiffman & L. E. Davis (Eds.), *Ethnic issues in adolescent mental health* (pp. 53–72). Newbury Park, CA: Sage.

Phinney, J. S., & Rosenthal, D. A. (1992). Ethnic identity in adolescence: Process, context, and outcome. In G. R. Adams, T. P Gullotta, & R. Montemayor (Eds.), *Adolescent identity formation* (pp. 145–172). Newbury Park, CA: Sage.

Phinney, J. S., & Rotheram, M. J. (Eds.). (1987). *Children's ethnic socialization. Pluralism and development.* Newbury Park, CA: Sage.

Phinney, J. S., & Tarver, S. (1988). Ethnic identity search and commitment in Black and White eighth graders. *Journal of Early Adolescence, 8,* 265–277.

Pinderhughes, E. (1989). *Understanding race, ethnicity, and power: The key to efficacy in clinical practice.* New York: Free Press.

Ponterotto, J. G. (1988). Racial consciousness development among white counselor trainees: A stage model. *Journal of Multicultural Counseling and Development, 16,* 146–156.

Ponterotto, J. G. (1989). Expanding directions for racial identity research. *The Counseling Psychologist, 17,* 264–272.

Ponterotto, J. G. (1991). The nature of prejudice revisited: Implications for counseling intervention. *Journal of Counseling and Development, 70,* 216–224.

Ponterotto, J. G., & Casas, J. M. (1991). *Handbook of racial/ethnic minority counseling research.* Springfield, IL: Charles C Thomas.

Ponterotto, J. G., Casas, J. M., Suzuki, L. A., & Alexander, C. M. (1995). *Handbook of multicultural counseling.* Thousand Oaks, CA: Sage.

Ponterotto, J. G., & Pedersen, P. B. (1993). *Preventing prejudice: A guide for counselors and educators.* Newbury Park, CA: Sage.

Poston, W. S. C. (1990). The biracial identity development model: A needed addition. *Journal of Counseling and Development, 69,* 152–155.

Poussaint, A. F. (1984). Study of interracial children presents positive picture. *Interracial Books for Children BULLETIN, 15*(6), 9–10.

Pressley, S. A. (1994, August 22). The color of love. In a country transfixed by race, black-white couples turn to each other for support. *The Washington Post,* pp. B1, B4.

Ramos, J. D. (1990). Counseling internationally adopted children. *Elementary School Guidance and Counseling, 25,* 147–152.

Ramsey, P. G. (1987). Young children's thinking about ethnic differences. In J. S. Phinney & M. J. Rotheram (Eds.), *Children's ethnic socialization: Pluralism and development* (pp. 56–72). Newbury Park, CA: Sage.

Ranard, D. A., & Gilzow, D. F. (1989, June). The Amerasians. *In America: Perspectives on Refugee Resettlement,* Issue No. 4. Washington D.C.: Center for Applied Linguistics.

Reynolds, A. L., & Pope, R. L. (1991). The complexities of diversity: Exploring multiple oppressions. *Journal of Counseling and Development, 70,* 174–180.

Roberts, P. O., & Cecil, N. L. (1993). *Developing multicultural awareness through children's literature: A guide for teachers and librarians, grades K–8.* Jefferson, NC: McFarland & Co.

Rochman, H. (1993). *Against borders: Promoting books for a multicultural world.* Chicago: American Library Association.

Root, M. P. P. (1990). Resolving "other" status: Identity development of biracial individuals. *Women and Therapy, 9,* 185–205.

Root, M. P. P. (1992a). Back to the drawing board: Methodological issues in research on multiracial people. In M. P. P. Root (Ed.), *Racially mixed people in America* (pp. 181–189). Newbury Park, CA: Sage.

Root, M. P. P. (1992b). From shortcuts to solutions. In M. P. P. Root (Ed.), *Racially mixed people in America* (pp. 342–347). Newbury Park, CA: Sage.

Root, M. P. P. (Ed.). (1992c). *Racially mixed people in America*. Newbury Park, CA: Sage.

Root, M. P. P. (1992d). Within, between, and beyond race. In M. P. P. Root (Ed.), *Racially mixed people in America* (pp. 3–11). Newbury Park, CA: Sage.

Root, M. P. P. (1994). Mixed-race women. In L. Comas-Diaz & B. Greene (Eds.), *Women of color: Integrating ethnic and gender identities in psychotherapy* (pp. 455–478). New York: Guilford Press.

Rose, I. G. (1984). Growing up in interracial families: An Hispanic perspective on biracial, bicultural families. *Interracial Books for Children BULLETIN, 15*(6), 12.

Rosenberg, M. B. (1986). *Living in two worlds*. New York: Lothrop, Lee & Shepard Books

Rosenblatt, P. C., Karis, T. A., & Powell, R. D. (1995). *Multiracial couples: Black and white voices*. Thousand Oaks, CA: Sage.

Rotheram, M. J., & Phinney, J. S. (1987). Introduction: Definitions and perspectives in the study of children's ethnic socialization. In J. S. Phinney & M. J. Rotheram (Eds.), *Children's ethnic socialization: Pluralism and development* (pp. 10–28). Newbury Park, CA: Sage.

Ruiz, A. S. (1990). Ethnic identity: Crisis and resolution. *Journal of Multicultural Counseling and Development, 18,* 29–40.

Sandor, G. (1994, June). "The other" Americans. *American Demographics,* pp. 36–42.

Sebring, D. L. (1985). Considerations in counseling interracial children. *Journal of Non-White Concerns in Personnel and Guidance, 13,* 3–9.

Shackford, K. (1984). Interracial children: Growing up healthy in an unhealthy society. *Interracial Books for Children BULLETIN, 15*(6), 4–6.

Sherman, R. L. (1990). Intergroup confict on high school campuses. *Journal of Multicultural Counseling and Development, 18,* 11–18.

Simon, R. J., & Alstein, H. (1992). *Adoption, race, and identity: From infancy through adolescence*. New York: Praeger.

Simon, R. J., Alstein, H., & Melli, M. S. (1994). *The case for transracial adoption*. Washington, D.C.: American University Press.

Smith, L. (1961). *Killers of the dream*. New York: Norton.

Sommers, V. S. (1964). The impact of dual-cultural membership on identity. *Psychiatry, 27*, 332–344.

Spickard, P. R. (1989). *Mixed blood: Intermarriage and ethnic identity in twentieth-century America*. Madison: University of Wisconsin Press.

Spivey, P. (1984). Growing up in interracial families: Communicating is the key. *Interracial Books for Children BULLETIN, 15*(6), 11.

Staff (1994, September). SPLC wins settlement in Wedowee case. *SPLC Report*, pp. 1, 6.

Staff (1994, December). *Teaching Tolerance* wins family life award. *SPLC Report*, pp. 1, 6.

Steel, M. (1995, Spring). New colors: Mixed-race families still find a mixed reception. *Teaching Tolerance*, pp. 44–46, 48–49.

Steele, S. (1990). *The content of our character: A new vision of race in America*. New York: Martin Press.

Stephan, C. W., & Stephan, W. G. (1989). After intermarriage: Ethnic identity among mixed-heritage Japanese-Americans and Hispanics. *Journal of Marriage and the Family, 51*, 507–519.

Stonequist, E. V. (1937). *The marginal man: A study in personality and culture conflict*. New York: Russell & Russell.

Sue, D. W., Arredondo, P., & McDavis, R. J. (1992). Multicultural counseling competencies and standards: A call to the profession. *Journal of Counseling and Development, 70*, 484–486.

Sue, D. W., & Sue, D. (1990). *Counseling the culturally different: Theory and practice*. (2nd ed.). New York: Wiley.

Tajfel, H. (1970). Experiments in intergroup discrimination. *Scientific American, 223*(5), 96–102.

Tajfel, H. (Ed.). (1982). *Social identity and intergroup relations*. New York: Cambridge University Press.

Tan, A. (1989). *The joy luck club*. New York: Putnam.

Teicher, J. D. (1968). Some observations on identity problems in children of Negro-White marriages. *The Journal of Nervous and Mental Disease, 146*, 249–256.

Thernstrom, S. (Ed). (1980). *Harvard encyclopedia of American ethnic groups*. Cambridge, MA: Belknap Press of Harvard University.

Thompson, C. L., & Rudolph, L. B. (1992). *Counseling children* (3rd ed.). Pacific Grove, CA: Brooks/Cole.

Thornton, M. C. (1983). *A social history of a multiethnic identity: The case of Black Japanese Americans*. Unpublished doctoral dissertation, University of Michigan, Ann Arbor.

Thornton, M. C. (1992). The quiet immigration: Foreign spouses of

U. S. citizens, 1945–1985. In M. P. P. Root (Ed.), *Racially mixed people in America* (pp. 64–76). Newbury Park, CA: Sage.

Tucker, M. B., & Mitchell-Kernan, C. (1990). New trends in black American interracial marriage: The social structural context. *Journal of Marriage and the Family, 52*, 209–218.

Updike, D. (1992, January). The colorings of childhood—On the burdens, and privileges, facing my multi-racial son. *Harper's Magazine*, pp. 63–67.

U.S. Bureau of the Census. (1991, 111th ed.) *Statistical abstract of the United States*. Washington, D.C.: U.S. Department of Commerce.

U.S. Bureau of the Census. (1992). *Marital status and living arrangements: March 1992*, Current Population Reports, Series P20, No. 468, Washington D.C.: U.S. Government Printing Office.

U.S. Catholic Conference, Migration and Refugee Services. (1988, May). Amerasians: Coming "home" at last. *Refugees: Concern & Response.* pp. 1–2.

U.S. Department of Health and Human Services. (1987). *Vital statistics of the United States, Volume III—Marriage and divorce*. Hyattsville, MD: National Center for Health Statistics.

Vaughan, G. M. (1987). A social psychological model of ethnic identity development. In J. S. Phinney & M. J. Rotheram (Eds.), *Children's ethnic socialization: Pluralism and development* (pp. 73–91). Newbury Park, CA: Sage.

von Sternberg, B. (1995a, April 12). 'Biracial' doesn't mean one or the other. *Star Tribune*, pp. 1, 10A.

von Sternberg, B. (1995b, April 12). Redefining the races. Census categories are likely to change. *Star Tribune*, pp. 1, 10A.

Walton, J. R. (1987). Children and prejudice. In A. Thomas & J. Grimes (Eds.), *Children's needs: Psychological perspectives* (pp. 434–441). Washington, D.C.: National Association of School Psychologists.

Wardle, F. (1987). Are you sensitive to interracial children's special identity needs? *Young Children, 42*(1), 53–59.

Wardle, F. (1988a). *Interracial families and biracial children: How the child care program should respond.* (ERIC Document Reproduction Service No. ED 302 331).

Wardle, F. (1988b). *Supporting individual differences in the classroom.* (ERIC Document Reproduction Service No. ED 303 270).

Wardle, F. (1990). Who has ten fingers and light brown skin and likes to sing "Bingo?" Identity development of biracial children. *Dimensions, 18*(4), 24–25, 31.

Wardle, F. (1991). Interracial children and their families: How school social workers should respond. *Social Work in Education, 13,* 215–223.

Wardle, F. (1992a). Supporting biracial children in the school setting. *Education and Treatment of Children, 15,* 163–172.

Wardle, F. (1992b, March/April). Transracial and interracial adoption: The myth of cultural genocide. *Interrace,* pp. 29–31.

Wardle, F. (1993, April). Interracial families and biracial children. *Child Care Information Exchange,* pp. 45–48.

Wardle, F., & Baptiste D. A. (1988). Growing up biracially in America: The inalienable rights of biracial children. *Nurturing Today, 9*(4), 9, 21.

Washington, J. R. (1970). *Marriage in Black and White.* Boston: Beacon Press.

Wehrly, B. (1991). Preparing multicultural counselors. *Counseling and Human Development, 24*(3), 1–24.

Wehrly, B. (1995). *Pathways to multicultural counseling competence: A developmental journey.* Pacific Grove, CA: Brooks/Cole.

Weiss, M. J. (1994, October). Love conquers all. *The Washingtonian,* pp. 98–99, 101–103, 135–137.

Wheeler, D. L. (1993, September 15). Black children, White parents: The difficult issue. *The Chronicle of Higher Education,* pp. A8–9, 16.

Wijeyesinghe, C. (1992). Towards an understanding of the racial identity of bi-racial people: The experience of racial self-identification of African-American/Euro-American adults and the factors affecting their choices of racial identity. *Dissertation Abstracts International, 53-11-A,* 3808A.

Williams, G. H. (1995). *Life on the color line. The true story of a White boy who discovered he was Black.* New York: Dutton.

Wilson, T. P. (1992). Blood quantum: Native American mixed bloods. In M. P. P. Root (Ed.), *Racially mixed people in America* (pp. 108–125). Newbury Park, CA: Sage.

Winn, N. N., & Priest, R. (1993). Counseling biracial children: A forgotten component of multicultural counseling. *Family Therapy, 20,* 29–36.

Wolfman, I. (1991). *Do people grow on family trees? Genealogy for kids & other beginners.* New York: Workman.

INDEX

A

Acceptance. *See also* Self-acceptance
  in adolescence, 75, 129
  of child
    by families of both races, 44–45
  in counseling adults, 129–130
  social
    in adolescence, 75
  of socially assigned identification, 121–122
  struggle for, 112
Adolescence. *See* Adolescents;
  Preadolescence
Adolescents
  acceptance and, 75, 129
  in adoptive homes, 101–103
  Alipura on biracial college-age, 83–86
  anger of
    in counseling process, 35–36
  biracial identity development of
    assessments in, 78
    conflicts in, 78, 79–80
    defense mechanisms and coping
      strategies in, 78
    Kerwin model for, 53, 81–83
  counseling of
    family in, 38
    guidelines for, 98–100
    issues in, 100
    as task, 73
  counselor roles and, 89–100
    case example of, 89–90
    with school administrators, 90–91
    with teachers, 91–95
  developmental tasks versus racial
    identity development in, 76, 77–81

  in foster homes, 100–101
    insecurity and rejection feelings of,
      100–101
  Gibbs' research on biracial, 77–81
  integration of dual/multiple heritages,
    95–96
  issues for, 74–76
    dating, 74–75
    label selection, 75–76
    racism, 75
    social acceptance, 75
    social forces, 76
  mental health assessment of, 95
    age-appropriate, nonproblem
      behaviors in, 96–97
    parental and family attitudes in, 97
    school and community resources in, 97
    social networks and peer relationships
      in, 97–98
  mixed heritage ethnic identity of
    Stephan and Stephan research on,
      82–83
  peer group and prejudice and, 77
    Phinney and associates ethnic identity
      model for, 86–89
    psychosocial adjustment of, 81
    racial/cultural/ethnic identity
      development of, 22–23, 76–89
Adoptees
  Black and Black-White
    discrimination in White
      neighborhoods/schools, 168–169
    self-identification of family and, 169
    of White parents, 101, 102, 168
    transracial, 170–171
    teacher expectations of, 102